Noodlin'
Steelhead
&
Salmon

Dick Swan

Frank Amato

PORTLAND

About this Book

I t isn't often that an angler finds himself in a brand new fishery, where his proven methods for taking "educated," pond—reared, lunker rainbow trout become the most popular methods for taking river steelhead in the Great Lakes.

It isn't often that an angler can butt-in on an already "traditional" Great Lakes trolling (meat) fishery and demonstrate that his charter clients land 95 to 100 percent of their Chinook salmon on six pound test monofilament, while others continue to land 50 percent on 30 pound test mono.

I am fortunate to be this angler! While Great Lakes steelheaders and West Coast steelheaders are a world apart, we both share in keeping hatchery fish to eat. However, because of the steelhead pressure from our surrounding eight states and Ontario, the vast majority of our steelhead are hatchery fish. Because of this, plus our more diversified steelhead sites, we "box" thousands more fish than coastal steelheaders.

There is now 32 years of on-the-stream evidence—from Washington's Cowlitz River to New York's Salmon River...and 15 years of on-the-lake evidence. This book will guarantee more hook-ups and prove to be the most sporting approach to our Great Lakes fishery.

Published in 1996 by Frank Amato Publications, Inc.
PO Box 82112, Portland, Oregon 97282. (503) 653-8108

Softbound ISBN: 0-57188-047-X
Printed in Canada

1 3 5 7 9 10 8 6 4 2

Noodlin' Steelhead-Salmon
Table of Contents

Acknowledgements

No man, married and with four children, could fish steelhead every weekend, every spring, for 14 years and not strain his marriage. I also never missed a day during our school's spring break. To adhere to such a strict steelhead discipline could put my desire in the "addiction" category. However, during these years of steelhead strain, many trips included the entire family—my wife Charleen ("Chuck"), sons Cole and Kurt, daughters Jaymie and Jill. At other times, just Cole and Kurt, or Jaymie and Jill would tag along. While none of them were actually into fishing, I could hand them the bending rod and they would land the fish, on two to four pound test mono. Instead of fishing, the boys tossed foot balls or baseballs while the girls would just be girls. Besides their common attention to our Labrador, Chip, food was also a common denominator among the four.

What an amazing turn-around took place when I resigned from education in 1976. From that time on, Chuck was on my back when I *wasn't* fishing! She knew how our rods sold when others saw them bending on the river.

My solo and family trips would result in meeting many of the same streamside faces which, over the years, developed into very close friendships. These friendships resulted in eight people getting involved with me as my noodle rod ambassadors on our Michigan rivers. All they were expected to do was answer questions about the rods and catch steelhead.

These eight steelheaders ranked "best of show" on our Michigan rivers. Their individual expertise not only gained the respect of Michigan's weekend crowds, but their individual techniques greatly benefited our steelheaders.

These eight, who wore the Swan Rod fishing vest, deserve special mention: Tom Janson was also a teacher who made the Betsie River a weekend habit. He taught Biology and Conservation at Meridian High School, while living in Midland.

His knowledge and application of techniques for steelhead,

not to mention his 6'4," 225 pound frame, made him a natural among the crowds of steelheaders. It was Tom who talked me into making his limber bicycle flag pole into the first Bike Rod. This rod would touch end-to-end with two pound test.

Tom took the rod on the Platte River and landed a new I.G.F.A. world record steelhead in the two pound test class. He later broke his own record with another steelhead, again, with his now famous Bike Rod. Tom was killed in an auto collision in the summer of 1987.

Ellis McColley was the first die-hard steelheader I met on the Elk River. He was also the stepdad of a football player I coached at Bullock Creek High School. He was the most tenacious outdoor sportsman I knew with several state shooting championships, in singles and doubles, skeet and trap. He ranked second in several state bowling meets.

With such a drive to meet any challenge it is little wonder his concentration at our Michigan surf fishing sites resulted in his pioneered techniques continuing to get the job done today. Ellis died while on an elk hunt in 1982.

Burl Brown came on to the steelhead scene at the Betsie River, where his down-home Okie style won the crowd over. Burl was a high school principal at the time, so with all of his traits he fit into our bunch just fine.

I will never forget the afternoon he came into my basement and tossed a package of spawn sacs at me. "What do you think?" he quickly asked. My first thought was, "What is he doing putting spawn sacs in a plastic bag?" A closer look proved they were made of plastic. Burl's Gold Nuggets became the first plastic spawn on the market. "Buck" Ryder first showed up at the Betsie wearing black leather and long hair. He was accompanied by two other bikers. We began to wonder what strange bed fellows these steelhead create.

Continued weekend trips made him a regular, except he concentrated his efforts at night with a lantern. His obvious steelhead success made him another one of the boys and he became my Detroit area connection.

I had just moved to Clare when I began hearing more about

Archie Sweet—the man who invented bobber fishing for steelhead at Tippy Dam. One evening he brought his dad to the house to ask about repairing a rod. After a few more visits from his home in next-door Farwell, he became my Tippy Dam connection. No one can carry his lunch when it comes to steelheading with bobbers. His old C.B. handle was appropriately, "Bobber Man."

Marty Vanderploeg was a student of Janson's, even though Marty attended Midland High School. Marty made the "Michigan Outdoors" television show when Tom introduced him to steelhead fishing on the Betsie. This is when cameraman Howard Shelly caught Marty landing his first steelhead—a 14 pounder. Marty was too young to drive and Tom saw to it that that would not keep him off the stream. I later asked Marty to join Tom and the rest of us, wearing a Swan Rod vest.

Mike Verburkmoes was also a teenager who began showing up at the Betsie on weekends. His mother would drive him from nearby Mesick each Friday evening, dropping him off at Homestead Dam, along with his tent. She would return Sunday evening to take him home.

I would make sure Mike had all of the necessary swivels, shot and hooks. His natural touch in hooking and fighting these silver bullets turned the heads of many veterans. Mike still exhibits the smoothest, most effortless, hook-setting technique on a river.

When I took the football job at Evart High School, in 1957, Tom Young lived across the street. Our common interest in fishing rainbows had us spending countless hours on the big river that ran through town, the Muskegon River. After I left Evart we still put in our time on the river together, so when steelhead made their comeback I made sure Tom was in on the Swan Rod Team.

With Ontario steelheaders really getting into their fishery, I recently added four enthusiastic Canadian river rats to the Swan Rod roster.

Leon Lambkin resides in Sarnia and as a fishing rep he keeps tabs on the hot rivers throughout the province. He specializes in the float technique and sports a 20 foot IMX graphite on their rivers.

John Perz is also located in Sarnia and assaults the Maitland River often. He bounces bottom and also fishes a float. These two techniques require a variety in style of cork handles and rod lengths with which he makes a spectacle of himself, punishing fish.

Wayne Ruston lives in Windsor but is in touch daily with what is happening on the Saugeen and Sable Rivers, located in South Hampton and Sable, Ontario. It is not unusual for Wayne to take off from work when he hears steelhead are in. He prefers fishing two pound test on 12 foot rods and has the knack to interest others in listening to him preach the lite-lining gospel.

Guy Therrien is not only from Windsor, he is Wayne's constant fishing partner and brother-in-law. Guy is the silent one, except when it comes to talking steelhead. Otherwise, his doubled over 11 1/2 foot noodle rod does his the talking for him.

He also has a 20 foot boat from which he and Wayne troll noodle rods for Lake St. Clair walleyes. This keeps him warmed up after work, waiting for the weekend steelhead trips up north.

These four Swan Rod steelheaders are (already into my winter show schedule) assisting me in preaching our noodle rod, lite-lining techniques at Canadian and Detroit sport shows. I owe my home family and my river family for hanging in there with me!

In the Beginning

Chapter 1

While many youngsters are tutored on fishing by their fathers, I was broken in by my oldest brother, Jay. It wasn't that my dad didn't fish, he just didn't fish as often as Jay.

Jay was a fly fishing purist, concentrating his efforts on largemouth bass. After all, what other game fish did an angler have a crack at while growing up in Gary, Indiana? This was back in 1938 when his fishing program was casting Bass Poppers and Hair-Frogs among lily pads.

Upon graduating from Emerson High School in 1939 his job at U.S. Steel earned him a Plymouth coupe and the beginning of many more trips to his favorite site, Mink Lake, near Valporaiso, Indiana. His 4:00 a.m. tap on my shoulder had me flying out of bed in anticipation of watching a bass slam the fly, going airborne, then released when boated. Jay was ahead of his time, not only in the catch and release ethic but in altering his fly rod to meet his demands. These are things never forgotten, especially for a eight year old.

My fishing duty was to row the rented boat, keeping Jay within casting range of the pads and broadside to his target. Another was cleaning and waxing his floating line when we arrived home.

During late morning, when bass were off their surface program, he would give me casting instructions with his 8 1/2 foot bamboo rod. Jay was a right-handed caster and although I am a lefty I learned to cast right-handed. Since he shot line from his left hand he retied the stripper guide slanting it to the left. This, plus learning to handle an 8 1/2 foot rod at such a young age, served me well in later years. His off-set stripper guide later became the basis for tying the Swan Twist guide arrangement on my trolling rod. The ease of casting his long fly rod initiated my desire for long rods.

In 1942 Jay enlisted in the Air Force and piloted a B24 Liberator in the South Pacific. My brother Phil enlisted and flew a B17 out of England and brother Jim also enlisted in the Air Force, but being color-blind he was grounded.

During the war Jay's fly rod was retired, so I bought a 9 foot telescoping metal fly rod. Living just a few houses from 5th Avenue (U.S. 12 & 20), it was convenient to hop the Gary bus to Miller to fish the lagoon in Marquette Park. One evening a bass sucked in my Hair-Frog but I popped the gut leader setting the hook. I was so excited I was up at 5:00 a.m. to catch the first bus to the lagoon, determined to even the score.

Later, in high school, I purchased a hard-to-find 7 foot casting rod blank. It was the first of many thousands of rod-blanks which would later pass through my fingers. After fitting it with a pistol grip I bought the (1947) revolutionary Shakespeare President casting reel, the first to feature nylon gears. I spent more time casting to the tournament rings, set up in the lagoon, than casting lures to bass.

During the war years I got involved with another type of fishing when I teamed up with a school chum, Don Kepshire, to help Howard Westerman, a commercial fisherman. Howard fished out of Sabinski's Fish House on the Gary beach of Lake Michigan. We fished gill nets for perch and herring out of a 17 foot, double oar-lock boat. "Kep" and I took great pride in our oarsmanship whenever we rowed Howard out to set or run nets.

After helping Howard for nine years, I became one mean fish cleaner. This included boning hundreds of pounds of herring with my thumb. It was also the time when I saw my first steelhead, caught in our large mesh floater net. Augie\ Sabinski and Howard called them "salmon." Before Howard died in 1989 he was most certain to learn the difference between the two fish.

From the commercial aspect of gill netting southern Lake Michigan I was a part of the demise of perch stocks and the extinction of herring. Augie and George Sabinski closed the Fish House in 1953 and Howard moved his operation to Burns Harbor.

After the war Jim returned home. Phil, surviving 35 bombing missions over Germany, made it home unscathed. Jay was killed in June of 1945 while taking off with a full load of bombs meant for the oil fields in Borneo. His bamboo fly rod remains retired.

During these summers my high school girlfriend, Charleen "Chuck" Fuhrman, would head to Cable, Wisconsin to spend the summer with her folks and aunt on Hammill Lake. I would visit to fish walleyes and plate size crappies.

Trolling June Bug spinners, tipped with nightcrawlers, for walleyes and tight-lining minnows for crappies were very effective techniques. I always tight-lined crappies with my fly rod. I let the fish pull the entire tip section under water before setting the hook. I never missed a crappie—crappies up to 18 inches. Aside from such outings, fishing took a back seat to athletics during high school.

In my senior year, 1948, I played in only four football games scoring five T.D.'s, which included two against Indiana's number one ranked team, Muncie Central. It earned me First Team, All-State football honors on two of three polls. This brought football scholarship offers from Michigan, Northwestern, Kentucky and an appointment to the Army.

In December I signed a Letter of Intent to play football for "Bear" Bryant. This was his first year at Kentucky. As fate would have it, I ended up playing basketball at Kentucky instead. Because it was the "Bear's" first year, Rupp ruled the roost and would not let me play football, or baseball.

I transferred to Indiana where Branch McCracken

allowed me to play both of the other sports. I believe I am the only basketball player who played with two N.C.A.A. National Champions at two universities. These teams included seven All-Americans.

It wasn't until my junior year that something hit home telling me Health, Physical Education and Recreation was where I should remain. It was also the year our Wyoming game steered me straight into the coaching game.

During the 1951-52 basketball season we had no All-Americans on the floor; however, Don Schlundt and Bobby Leonard would win that honor the following season, as the National Champions.

We were ranked fifth in the nation and Wyoming, playing with one All-American, was also ranked. The Cowboys were thinking big and selected our game to dedicate their new fieldhouse.

Sammy Esposito, who scored a game high 81 points at Chicago's Fenger High School and who later joined the White Sox, bumped Sam Miranda, a senior from Collinsville, Illinois from his starting guard position. "Espo" and I were the second and third athletes at I.U. to win a sweater in football, basketball and baseball. Miranda was our dribbling specialist who closed each practice session going 1-on-2, keeping the ball away from the two.

The hype from the dedication kept the fire lit under the Cowboys and the thin air was wearing on us and our lead. In the closing seconds, Miranda was sitting next to me on the bench. There was still no indication McCracken was going to put him in to dribble the game away.

I was getting hot! I reached over and began pulling on Miranda, yelling, "Get in there, get in there." Sam would pull back saying, "I can't go in!" I kept pulling and yelling until I knew McCracken heard me. The bench knows I got Miranda into the game where he did his thing, winning the game by a point! While it helped kill my relationship with McCracken it sure boosted me into wanting to coach.

Today, the only active team member I played with at Kentucky is C.M. Newton, Athletic Director at Kentucky. At Indiana, Bobby Leonard became the first coach of the Indianapolis Pacers, but was released many years ago.

The only fishing I can remember doing at I.U., was when three of us from South Hall (dormitory) bought minnows and headed for some bridge to fish crappies. I proposed we have a contest with whose fish could pull the bobber the longest distance, before setting the hook. I don't remember who won, but we sure did see some fish going 20 to 30 yards. I do remember we ate our catch on a hot plate in the basement of the dorm.

After graduating from Indiana in 1953, Chuck and I were married on a 104 degree day, June 20. By now I had her casting a 6 foot Shakespeare rod with a Marhof casting reel. However, her honeymoon instructions included leaving the fishing tackle home during our trip to Paw Paw, Michigan.

After a boring next morning, she mentioned she wished I would have brought the fishing gear, at which time I opened the trunk of the car and presto!

My brother Phil was a field engineer, surveying a site at the Coke (coal) Plant, at U.S. Steel and I was the "rodman" on the survey crew. He also got into the fishing mode very quickly, with us making frequent trips to the Kankakee River bayous at Momence, Illinois. The program was fishing Golden Roach minnows and bobbers for huge Northerns. It was rare to land one of these brutes because of the vegetation, but what horrendous hits.

The job and fishing trips were to cease for me in September of 1953, when I jumped on a train, along with many of my Gary buddies, to begin serving time in the Army at Ft. Riley, Kansas.

1954 - Endcoach, Fort Carson "Mountaineer" Football Team

The Colorado Experience
Chapter 2

During those formative years in Gary, and while in college, I made a steady diet of consuming hunting and fishing articles published in the "big three" outdoor magazines. I read them cover to cover, including the ads. I could never get used to looking at pictures of a small trout,with its blunt, tiny head. It looked odd, compared to the warm water species to which I was accustomed.

After finishing 16 weeks of training at Ft. Riley, I was transferred to Camp Carson near Colorado Springs, Colorado.Like the Army, looking at these trout took some getting used to before they started looking like real fish. Even cleaning a small trout was very different and much faster. For the first time I didn't have to scale the fish.

After arriving at Carson, my athletic background helped me get assigned to the fieldhouse where I worked with the late great Billy Martin and his famous "Baby Blue"Cadillac. I also became end coach for the post football team. This included coaching John Tracy, who became an All-American at Texas A.&M., under the "Bear." Later, I also became head basketball coach, coaching Jed Domeyer before he returned to the University of Minnesota, where he led the Big Ten in scoring.

With Lt. Chet Lukawski just moving in as Sports Officer,I had it made in the shade. Chet was from East Chicago and was at Kentucky with me, where he later played in three bowl games under the "Bear." The two of us, along with the late Jim "Moose" McKenzie, also from Gary and also on those three bowl teams with Chet, were the "dynamic trio" on Kentucky's campus. Jim was later named head football coach at the University of Oklahoma, but died of a heart attack before his first game.

My daily routine in the fieldhouse was keeping it "spit and polished" and checking out recreational equipment to the troops. The equipment included fishing tackle, with 7 1/2 foot Langley fly rods.

M/Sgt. Ed Eastman not only posted my fieldhouse schedule but became my mentor for deer hunting and trout fishing. When Chuck joined me in Colorado Springs, Ed and his wife,"Butch," made it a hunting-fishing foursome.

The girls slept in Ed's Nash Ambassador, while he and I pitched our G.I. shelter-halves. We all had our mountain sleeping bags and 7 foot fly rods. There was no problem catching enough small trout to eat, but getting into the big rainbows was another story.

While in the fieldhouse, whenever a trooper checked in a fly rod, I would ask the obvious questions about how he did and where. When this one guy told about catching an 18 inch rainbow, I was all ears. He finally got around to mentioning the place, Rainbow Falls, just a short drive over our back-yard mountain, Pike's Peak. He qualified the site as a commercial pond where rainbows were raised for restaurants.It was "pay for your catch" for anglers. Since I had not hooked a big rainbow yet, I was there on the weekend.

He was right about the pond being loaded with lunker rainbows. I was sure I had it made. After all, I didn't have a problem catching their little brothers.

Well, I got skunked. I would either spook them or they would insult me by ignoring my fly or bait. Some would hesitate and take a second look, then continue on their way.Dry fly, wet fly, crawler, or worm, it didn't make a difference to these wise old veteran 'bows. All of this, plus having visible trout swimming freely in a pond, instead of holding in the current of a stream, was another ball game to learn.

I began thinking, these bigger 'bows, in spite of their size, may require the same small leaders and bait as their smaller stream cousins. Upon deciding to adopt the small trout approach, I began by opting for a jar of Atlas salmon eggs and a spool of two pound test leader.

When I next graced the pond, I took a handful of salmon eggs and after spotting some bigger fish, I liberally seeded the water. I could not believe how they scarfed up the eggs. Wow! Feeling sure of myself, I nailed an egg on the hook and a small split shot on the leader—no luck. It was time to start over.

Next time I tossed in only one egg, so I could concentrate more on their reaction. As the egg free-floated down, a 'bow would swim past it, turn quickly, scrutinize the action of the egg, then inhale it. Talk about selective feeding!

I tied on another two pound leader without the tiny split shot. Now, in order to have the egg stay on the hook while fly casting, I had to raise my arm, lock the elbow and false cast from the shoulder in a smooth "windmill" motion.

With the egg surviving the cast, I watched a big rainbow perform its discriminating ritual. As it turned to eyeball the egg, I tensed! The trout calmly turned and swam away. The egg obviously did not pass the test. It was back to the sport shop.

With everything else downsized, I had to give serious consideration to hook size. I looked for the smallest egg hook possible and came up with one I could bury completely in the salmon egg. As far as I could see, I now had all the bases pretty well covered—except the 7 foot flyrod.

The next day, I asked Ed if he knew anyone coming from Korea with a bamboo fly rod. He called a guy who had one and set up a time to meet in the fieldhouse. It was the usual 9footer I heard about, with an extra fly tip and a bamboo casting rod. It was packed nicely in the usual wooden box. I bought it new for $5.00.

Saturday found me at the pond bright and early. I rigged the 9 foot rod with a 9 foot, two pound test leader. I buried the tiny hook in an egg, then made the necessary windmill cast to deliver the egg. I watched a rainbow swim by it, turn to inspect it, then move in and gulp! It was something to see and feel.

In the next three hours of fishing I learned the importance of the soft windmill delivery. If the eye of the hook did not remain buried in the egg, forget it. Also,after releasing some real beauties, I took home a 22 inch rainbow. It seemed only fitting these "restaurant" fish would end up on our dining room table. Needless to say, the9 foot fly rod and two pound leaders, with egg hooks, would unknowingly set the stage for a similar challenge seven years later.

An early June releasefrom the Army in 1955 sent Chuck back to Gary to work and me back to Bloomington, to begin my summers working on a M.S. degree. I had to work on my degree during the summers because I was lucky enough to get a Drivers Education position at Gary Edison and Wirt High Schools. I taught a half-day a teach school. This began my teaching career.

Northern Canada's Steelhead
Chapter 3

After leaving a Drivers Education position in the Gary School District, I moved to Michigan where I coached my way to Midland Bullock Creek High School in 1962. It was a new high school district, opening with students up to the 10th grade. I was the only coach, hiring more the next year. Finally, with a full complement of coaches, I remained as head football coach and athletic director. By now I had become acquainted with many of the dads, including a few who were stream fishermen.

During the season, one halfback's dad, Roy Devereaux, told me of his trips to Canada's Lake Superior streams for steelhead. I was pleasantly shocked to hear this, since I thought their steelhead fishery went down the tubes along with Michigan's because of the sea lamprey. Roy's info was detailed so I was ready for Canada's spring opener.

Because of Lake Superior's cold temperatures and Canada's snow base, steelhead runs didn't peak until the second week of May. However, I began traveling at the end of April hitting the Stokely, Pancake, Chippewa, Montreal and Speckled Trout Creek. If fishing was slow I would continue to the Agawa and Sand rivers.

It became common knowledge that lamprey stocks did not reach the magnitude in Lake Superior as in the other Great Lakes; therefore, steelhead were not wiped out. Nevertheless an electric lamprey weir was installed on the Pancake River.

When the weir was not in operation, it became a popular fishing site. However, since it was also one of the rare streams to color up with run-off, it never appealed to me. Other streams survived coloring due to heavy forests reaching to their banks.

From an economic standpoint, crossing the Mackinaw Bridge was the biggest expense. Yes, the $7.50 round trip toll was more than the gasoline tab. With a cooler full of sandwiches and my G.I. mountain sleeping bag, eating and sleeping was no problem.

A 9 foot Shakespeare fly rod, with a six inch fighting butt, was added to my stream arsenal. Naturally, it was the longest fly rod on the market. I stripped the rod and rebuilt it as a combination spin-fly rod. The fighting butt made it the perfect closed-face spinning rod. The larger spinning guides made it a more functional fly rod, shooting fly line farther because of less rod slap and less constriction through the larger guide rings. Once again, Jay's rod modification reminded me manufacturers don't fish enough. While this long, white Wonder Rod had the usual parabolic rod action, it wasn't soft enough for two pound test leaders, I had to opt

The "Hex" fly, or giant mayfly, nymph (wiggler) is a popular live bait fished by Michigan steelheaders.

Noodlin' Steelhead-Salmon

for four pound test.

The South Bend closed-face reel was my dad's and still worked like new. I started spin fishing with a closed-face because it is the only type of casting reel which can be handled like a fly reel. I am lost without handling the line and open-face reels make it too difficult.

One weekend on the Stokely, I met a steelheader from St. Charles, Michigan, who showed me his favorite hook, an Eagle Claw, style 30 wide bend, in sizes 12 and 14. He convinced me of its pluses and I picked some up when I returned to Midland. He also showed me his favorite bait, bugs, or wigglers. A wiggler is the nymph of our giant "Hex" fly, the Hexagenia lambata.

During the two years I fished these streams, Speckle Trout Creek became my favorite. The water spilling over the small falls offered protection to steelhead, as did the hole located at the bend below the falls. It was great to sit on the edge of the falls and assist the migrating leapers back into the water, whenever their jumps caused them to get dry- docked. I fished the rod in one hand and pushed steelhead back into the current with the other.

These first experiences with steelhead were real eye openers. Most characteristics I witnessed were never seen in print, while much of what I did read was not applicable to Lake Superior steelhead in this environment. It was obvious the written word should be rewritten.

American steelheaders I talked to in Canada never really "killed" the steelhead in these small streams. Their philosophy was, if they hooked a few and landed one or two, it made the trip worthwhile. This philosophy became the name of the steelheading game.

Michigan's Renovated Steelhead Runs

A s in other fields, my position at school required a discipline in scheduling, establishing priorities, etc. I also had to fit in with the daily activities of staff and students. Such daily routines also seemed to have set the pace during my time outside of school.

In spite of having three rug-rats around the house, I would take time to hunt small game and deer before and after school and on weekends. The only sport lacking my time was fishing steelhead, which was limited to only weekends and holidays. In an attempt to fill any void, I would spend hours engrossed in my two "bibles," Herter's and Finnysport catalogs. The unique adventures of George and Jacques, printed as endorsements for particular items, caused me to favor Herter's.

Another priority was the weekly schedule of watching "Michigan Outdoors" on Thursday night at 7:00, with Mort Neff. He and his camera crew would zero in on places to go before a particular season opener. Needless to say, I was glued to the tube the night he covered steelhead showing up in our Lake Superior streams. With runs already occurring in Canadian streams, it was only a matter of time before substantial runs would hit our shoreline of Lake Superior.

I say "substantial" because steelhead never really thrived on our side of Lake Superior. It was Lake Michigan steelhead caught in our rivers in the 1940s, which earned world record recognition in Field & Stream magazine.

Mort's positive report sounded like a new generation of steelhead must have moved in. While this news caused me to stop traveling to Canada, it didn't prevent my paying the toll to cross the "Big Mac" bridge. However, it required traveling only one spring to the Upper Peninsula's Huron, Falls, Silver, Slate and Ravine rivers, to know Canadian streams were way ahead of our runs of Lake Superior steelhead.

The picture changed the following spring as I began to hear about steelhead in Lake Michigan streams. Then Mort showed films of the Elk River loaded with steelhead. This was to be the start of a long romance with this most noble trout.

The Elk is one of the most critical steelhead streams in Michigan, demanding finesse fishing par excellence for consistent hookups.

I rate the Elk, located in Elk Rapids, Michigan, as our second shortest steelhead stream second to the Leland River, in Leland, Michigan. Elk River originates at the small power dam which belches its water from Elk Lake into the East Arm of Traverse Bay.

It didn't take too many steelheaders gathering at this limited site to form a crowd. Since I was alone on my trips, it was easier for me to develop the practice of rising early enough to get to my hot spot on the river about an hour before day break. It became a case of first come-first served.

I had already learned it wasn't worth the effort to fish steelhead in the dark, so I would just stand in place waiting

Our normal size spawn bag contained eight to ten steelhead eggs, or three Chinook eggs.

for enough daylight to tie knots. As others arrived the typical steelhead conversations would begin. It was this type of communicating that developed friendships on a weekly basis and in most cases, for a lifetime.

Elk River, with its deep water and fast current near the dam, offered a different challenge than those shallower rivers farther north. The difference became obvious with each hooked fish. It also became humorous, as the belly in the line was so great, whenever a fish hit, its immediate jumps could not be detected in the rod. It wasn't until the bowed line straightened that the lucky angler could yell a belated "fish on." This served as my first lesson in the importance of line control for deep water lunkers.

Just below the deeper water the Elk shallows up dramatically, offering steelheaders a gravel spawning area to fish. It was sight fishing at its best, with the adult fish holding steady in the current. The smallness of the Elk is unique in itself, but having two distinct fishing areas is amazing.

Fishing spawning steelhead in Michigan began largely because in the early 1960s the law was changed to allow the use of real fish eggs for bait. Before the change sponge was the preferred bait. With this change and being able to see bedding steelhead, Michigan steelheaders were the first to establish loose steelhead eggs, tied in a nylon bag, as bait. It quickly became the number one steelhead bait. The size of these Lake Michigan steelhead was a real eye- opener. Having been accustomed to seeing six pounders from Lake Superior, these 8 to 12 pound fish were something else. They were not only longer, but deeper. We all understood Lake Superior remains colder, keeping their fish down-sized, but the size difference earned special attention nonetheless. It was also interesting to note the number of steelhead wearing metal tags in their jaw. These fish proved to be Wisconsin plants.

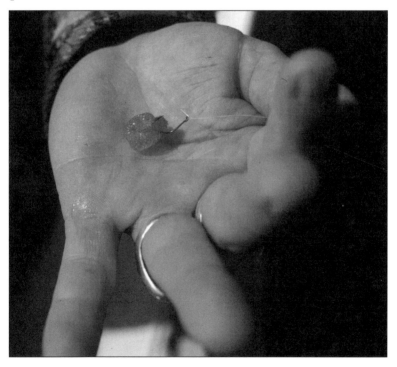

Our streamside conversations always included what we had heard about other steelhead runs and each week the names of more rivers were mentioned. However, along with the new names being added, one river was regularly talked about—the Betsie River.

After our spring run fish faded in the Elk River, I took a scouting trip to the Betsie to get a picture of what I had heard about. It too was different, offering another challenge. I found myself sitting on the north abutment of Homestead Dam on the March opener.

Like the Elk, this Betsie steelhead site operated on a first come-first served basis and like the Elk late-comers eventually swarmed onto the river. However, unlike the Elk, about 30 of us were sitting hip-to-hip on the big north cement abutment. How is that for togetherness?

Also, unlike the Elk, each of us had only six to eight foot drifts, straight down. Short rods or long rods it made no difference when drifting bait straight below you. Spinning reels, or fly reels, it made no difference when dropping a line below you. Of course, if you were a steelhead enthusiast who could not handle the closeness of sitting hip-to-hip you could always go downstream and stand shoulder-to-shoulder. Either way, friends made on Betsie River became very close friends.

The Betsie offered steelhead vast areas of spawning gravel. It was not uncommon to nail a Betsie spring spawner weighing in at 14 pounds. If it was a female it could furnish a steelheader enough eggs to last two seasons.

As in every crowd steelhead reports from other rivers were of great interest, generating a barrage of questions to the angler offering the report. On rivers the length of the Betsie even reports coming from downstream anglers were of interest. There was never a lack of communications among steelheaders, strangers or not.

After spending a few springs with the sleek-bodied Lake Superior steelhead, these Lake Michigan "footballs" were a real eye-opener.

These early birds get the worm; it is important to get the top two positions on the north and middle wall of Homestead Dam on the Betsie River.

Among the rivers mentioned most in those reports was the Big Manistee River, Tippy Dam in particular. One of the fishing facts in Michigan is that there is usually a barrier on our rivers where migrating fish have to stop, or re-coup, before continuing on. Tippy Dam stops them. Therefore, steelheaders unfamiliar with these rivers need only to seek out the dam sites in order to locate fish. This is why more is heard about steelhead fishing on our rivers with dams than rivers without dams. This is not to suggest great steelhead fishing experiences occur only on rivers with dams. In fact, any water emptying into our Great Lakes can suck steelhead into it, including their tributaries, such as farmland drainage ditches.

Moving to Elk River, Betsie, then to Tippy Dam presented three very different steelhead sites. Any steelheader coming to Tippy for the first time stands in awe of this massive, intimidating fishery. On the current side of the dam stand the long-distant casters, while on the quiet water side row-boaters do their thing. A spillway (Coffer Dam) is located some 70 yards below the face of the dam. Water below the coffer is much shallower and holds bedding fish.

The greatest fishing pressure comes above the coffer on the south (current) side of the dam. While not as deep as the upper section of the Elk, longer casts into the fast current resulted in the same line control problem.

In spite of the physical challenges we must address on our many steelhead streams, the common denominator is spring steelhead. These are guaranteed annual runs because of our aggressive hatchery program. The spring run gene pool was set in cement—that is, until the mid-1960s, when word trickled down that a few steelhead were showing up at Tippy in the fall.

During the fall, no one could keep me from hunting partridge, pheasants, ducks, or geese. Steelhead time was in the spring. However, in October of 1966 I allowed two fellow teachers, Fred Warner and John Fuller, to talk me into visiting Tippy with them. I didn't recognize the site with all of the

North wall of Homestead Dam, Betsie River.

After steelheading on the small Canadian tribs of Lake Superior, then our Elk and Betsie rivers, the vast waters at Tippy Dam, on the Big Manistee River, loomed as the most intimidating steelhead site anywhere.

leaves on the trees and in fall colors. I felt out of place with a spawn bag ready to unload on a fall steelhead, instead of unloading No. 6 shot at a pheasant.

I delivered the spawn bag into my favorite springtime drifting lane and "fish on." It was a silver-plated female. I became a believer. There were fall steelhead to be caught without spring crowds, so I remained a fall hunter for a very short time.

Introducing Noodle Rods to Michigan Steelheaders
Chapter 5

Nineteen sixty-five was a most eventful year. After a dismal past football season and graduating our first senior class in June, I put extra demands on the returning players. They rose to the occasion, winning our new conference.

I also met Ellis McColley, stepdad to one of my tackles and we began meeting at Elk River. It became an every weekend occurrence where we would put on a clinic, hooking most of the steelhead.

I was still fishing the 9 1/2 foot Shakespeare Wonder Rod, but added another style closed-face reel, the Shakespeare 1810. Ellis had an 8 1/2 foot fly rod with a Johnson Century spin-cast reel mounted under the rod, instead of on top of it. We both ran long lengths of four pound test leaders. We shared a lot in common. As a result of my experience on the Betsie, it became a topic which had him meeting me on the North abutment the following March.

As I drove through Mesick, located 25 miles east of Homestead Dam, the local bank's temperature reading was eight degrees. Although this indicated ice would form in the rod guides, the clear sky indicated there should be sun too. Sunshine is very important in times of chilled river water. It works wonders warming water temperatures later in the morning or early afternoon. It only takes one or two degrees to snap a steelhead out of its lethargic state of being.

I was on the abutment when Ellis arrived. There was plenty of room because cold mornings quickly separate the fishermen from the sleepers. We caught each other up on what we both had heard from others and as day was break-

Hip-to-hip steelheading on the north wall of Homestead Dam, encouraged close friendships on the Betsie River. Big steelhead also encouraged the use of some big tackle.

ing, we put our rods together in preparation for the day.

By 10:30 a.m. the warm penetrating rays of the sun began having their effect on the chilly water. The sun also caused many others to assault the abutments. As they swarmed onto the three cement walls, I was into the first fish of the morning. A loud, "Fish on!" alerted those on the lower end of the wall and their lines quickly began to clear the water. The fish immediately exploded from the river and upon re-entry, it shot downstream in sheer panic. I put it in gear and began following the fish down the slanting wall, because when fishing in a crowd, the quickest way to lose a fish is to let it get too far from you and into the line of some unsuspecting angler fishing downstream.

With the long fly rod "maxed," the pressure caused the fish to slow as it neared the Cedar Hole. It began slugging it out with me, throwing its head back and forth in an attempt to rid its jaw of the nagging hook. After a few minutes of this fighting tactic, it began slip-sliding across the current toward me. It soon tipped over onto its silver flank and I slid the sleek six pounder up on the bank. I was to repeat this landing scenario two more times during the long day, while Ellis beached his third steelhead at 9:30 p.m..

There is nothing earth-shattering about two steelheaders landing six fish in one day. However, during the day Ellis and I had totaled 19 trips down the abutment, while not one other angler hooked a fish!

Among the throngs of people lining the three abutments, I saw one other fly rod along with other tackle ranging from traditional spinning gear to heavy duty saltwater tackle. Whenever fishing in such a crowd there are no secrets—no secret setups, etc. Every piece of tackle is hanging out there for others to glean. So what caused the difference in steelhead action during this day on the Betsie?

Those coming from a fly fishing background know the importance of leader selection. Spin fishers and bait casters know the importance of line selection. All of us know these requirements can differ, due to the environs (dirty water, snag-free water, etc.) and the species of fish being pursued. These requirements can also differ during the day and whether it is sunny or overcast.

However, when it comes to applying these notions to river steelhead and salmon we better first understand the fish. We need to understand its mental make-up when the fish finds itself in the shallow confines of a stream, instead of the safety of its deep lake environs, whether it is unmolested, holding in the current or dodging everything but the kitchen sink, being presented by a crowd of anglers.

Unfortunately, too many anglers ignore these conditions when approaching these rivers. Instead, they focus on the size of the fish in making their leader-line selection. Too many steelheaders get caught up in the "big fish, big tackle" syndrome when determining terminal tackle.

On the Betsie, Ellis and I were fishing the same leaders required to keep us into fish when we fished Elk River. Our choice of leaders was the sole determiner for our 19 hook-ups, just like terminal rigs are for others. Though we could identify others' rods and reels, it is more difficult to determine weight leaders. There is no question, the others were fishing leaders that were too heavy.

Regardless of the species, anglers should think like the fish they hope to hook, which, in this case, includes the spawn run "habits" of steelhead. For instance:

When Mother Nature forces this anadromous strain to leave the safety of their feeding grounds to enter the shallow, clear water confines of a stream, many physiological and mental changes occur. Food intake is no longer a body requirement, while their reproductive tracts continue to reach full development. Their bodies lay down an extra heavy ring of calcium on each scale, which is wider than their regular annual rings. Their need to spawn forces them to inhabit streams 24 hours a day, for the duration necessary to complete this stage of their lives. While on these shallow gravel redds, the fish remain exposed to their natural enemies, becoming fearful for their lives. Once again, crowds of anglers, tossing different concoctions of bait at these spawners also puts them on "red alert."

In my mind, to compensate I must present an offering that is less threatening to this fish. To be less threatening the leader must be less visible, which means it must be of clear color and thin diameter. On the Betsie and Elk this meant using four pound test leaders.

I think of some conglomerate impaled on a huge No. 2 hook on a collision course with the face of a lunker. Its visual acuity also allows the fish to see a large swivel and heavy lead trailing close behind (Northwest steelheaders preach 18" leaders). To compensate, I present a small spawn bag hanging from a No. 14 hook, with my swivel and lead six to ten feet behind. I tagged this long leader a "searching" leader. It can't get any less threatening than this. This is the terminal rig I drift successfully in low, slow, crystal-clear water—waters I label, "critical" water.

The Betsie was Tom Janson's pet river and the first bend was his honey-hole; therefore, it is little wonder he named his daughter "Betsie", and we named the first bend below the dam in his honor, "Janson's Bend."

In 1978, during our second summer trip to Washington, I was approached by an angler who asked if I could make their Trout Unlimited meeting in Willamette, Oregon. I checked with the guys and it was a go. On the morning of the meeting I landed a beautiful 15 pound torpedo on the usual searching leader. I told the guys I would keep it for one of the door prizes at the meeting.

When I was done with my presentation that night one of the questions from the group was about our long leaders. They are so accustomed to 18 inch leaders, he couldn't understand our hooking so many steelhead on our longer ones. First, I reminded him of the door prize I caught on this leader, then I proceeded to explain what goes on during the drift.

The leader won't begin to straighten out downstream until the weight hits bottom. Then, with each consecutive bump, each hesitation has the current pulling on the bait, straightening the leader ahead of the weight. Why else do 98 percent of the hook-ups come during the lower one-third of the drift?

No, a searching leader won't get the job done in fast water because it can't get down before the drift was completed. We don't like that type of water, even though a fast current sure helps to set a hook.

With long leaders it is not unusual to come off a snag and be into a steelhead. This occurs because, though the weight is hung up, the leader swings around behind the snag, into the maw of a fish resting in the quiet water.

By now all of my Swan Rod guys, except Archie, were also making the Betsie home base for steelhead. With talent like this coming together each weekend, it became natural to put some of this theory to the test. I mentioned it to Janson, and with Marty included, we selected the first bend of the river as our testing grounds. We agreed to spend three consecutive weekends on the bend. One would fish with two pound leaders, one with four pound and the other, six pound test. We stood together, rotating positions at intervals, all fishing the same bait. This experiment proved the difference in hook-ups between four and six pound test was like night and day. I guess we felt this would happen, because none of us ever carried six pound in our vests anyway. However, we did not find too wide a margin in hook-ups between two and four pound test, at least not enough to wager the outcome in a contest.

Along with this idea of a contest, this experiment of ours also gave Tom the audacity to challenge "Butch" Furtman, of Duluth, Minnesota. Now if you haven't heard of Butch, you have never fished the Betsie in March when the Duluth boys continue to make this steelhead trip. They catch their share of fish!

If you don't fish the Betsie when these members of the Lake Superior Steelheaders Association grace its banks, you should know they don't even come close to using 4 pound test, let alone two pound. Their superswift streams won't permit its use, so they stick with their program of fishing heavier artillery when fishing here.

Tom chose to go with two pound test in the contest against Butch. After traversing the banks of the river over a period of time they called it quits. If you ever heard Tom talk

Once understanding the need for finesse fishing, Marty, Bill Price, Bob Jane and I returned to the Platte. It was a frigid weekend and we were greeted with the challenge of drifting baits between ice flows.

about it, he "smoked 'em."

As we conducted this mono experiment on the bend of the Betsie, there was no way we could see the fish. The depth and surface current prevented it. So once again, everything that was taking place underwater could only register in my mind's eye. It wasn't until we got into Platte River coho that everything pictured in my mind finally came to light.

Our favorite time to hit the Platte was during winter, after the notorious New York snaggers and "lifters" returned home to their dens. This was also the time when the river was at its lowest and super clear. On each trip we would have a river full of spawning coho all to ourselves. Again, this was a perfect set-up for experimenting and once again it was Janson, Marty and me.

Using the same bait and two pound test we were looking for the effect various lengths of leader had on a bedding spawner. It was a real eye-opener, as the crystal water gave us the window to view the hi-visibility yarn fly along every inch of the drift. We viewed the fly drift high over their heads, with no response. We saw the fish move out of the way of the short leaders and

remain relaxed with the searching leaders. On one drift, we watched the fly come on target with a dorsal fin. Of course we experience foul hooked fish many times but to see it happen was something else.

Those early days of our Platte River coho runs were really a sight to behold. This was before Tempo Tech and Noble brought forth the commercial aspect of harvesting these fish.

Those days are gone, but hopefully with the present government investigation of Tempo Tech's operations in Michigan and New York, we will be rid of the commercial taking of these fish and give them back to the sport fisherman, for whom they were intended.

It is important to be willing to adjust to existing water conditions. Too often accepted traditional methods just won't get it done, especially under the critical water conditions just

mentioned. On the other hand, whenever you address a stream which is colored up from run-off water, be my guest and fish any technique you wish. Dirty water offers these spawners a great big security blanket, where they are as snug as a bug in a rug. This is the time when anything goes, even the kitchen sink.

After resigning from education, I was at Tippy every morning for two consecutive weeks. We had a big snow melt and the river was as dirty as it could get. The south side was shoulder-to-shoulder and again it featured fishing rods of the Howitzer class. The angler who was armed with the largest caliber rod was an old crippled man, sitting on a stool, as he tossed his "grenades" into the current.

Each morning, at about 10:30 the siren would sound, indicating the turbines would be going full blow in five minutes. This was my signal to hang it up for the day, since I never fish high water at Tippy. I enjoyed my usual number of hook-ups and on my way out I passed the long row of anglers. It appeared everyone, yes, even the old man, had steelhead on their stringer. It was like that the first few mornings of the week.

By the middle of the second week, the faces in the crowd changed and so did the clarity of the water. You guessed it! It cleared up to the point where I was one of the few who continued to enjoy hook-ups, while others stood practicing their casting.

Platte River Hatchery manager, Chuck Pecor (right), supervises Tempo Tech's coho harvest in October of 1981.

41

As a successful athlete and coach, I learned to never change a winning combination. Therefore, whether it is critical water or dirty water, I don't change my terminal rigging practices.

When I began guiding, I would start the early morning hours with the clients fishing four pound test leaders. As it grew lighter I switched to two pound. While I personally never started with four pound, I thought I would cut the clients a little slack with the extra poundage.

However, like any steelhead enthusiast should do on his drive back home, I began asking myself if there was anything else I could have done to get my clients more hook-ups. After all, I am the most expensive river guide in Michigan and I never fish four pound. Since I don't start them with four pound anymore, the answer to this self-searching, on-the-road question, has been "No, there is nothing more I can do for them."

I will never be sure if the four pound test made a difference, because 99 percent of my clients continue to hook at least one steelhead and 95 percent land at least one.

Fishing with two-four pound test terminal tackle is no different than an angler who chooses to fish with 12 pound test, because both must select a rod best designed to handle their choice of mono. Both must fish with "balanced" tackle.

Since the invention of fly fishing, each rod is designed to cast a certain weight fly line. Each fly rod has the weight listed. This ensures casting with balanced fly tackle. It becomes very noticeable when attempting to fly cast the wrong weight line.

Spinning rods may also list a range of recommended weight monofilament to use, but if the range exceeds a difference of six pounds, you will fish out-of-balance. It is impossible to "max" the same rod with two pound test and six pound. Either the two pound will break, or the rod will break with six pound.

It is my background in fly fishing and the neglect of specifying leader requirements for fly rods that had me develop the only rod which is designed to "max" with specific weight monofilament lines, or leaders—the noodle rod. However, even today there remains a misconception of "line versus leader"—is a noodle rod designed for the heavier eight pound monofilament main line we spool (the equivalent of fly line in this case), or the lighter two pound leader?

The eight pound main line spooled on a spin reel serves like the fly line, in that it will rarely break when fishing with a leader which is lighter. Since it is the lighter leader which will break first, the leader becomes the specific determiner for what rod action is needed, not the main line.

The noodle rod is nothing more than an extra long fly rod, with the good ol' parabolic, slow action, which allows the rod to bend down through the cork handle. It becomes a long shock absorber, protecting the light leaders. I "converted" this long fly rod, as I always have, for spin fishing too; however, the demand from spin fishers started me manufacturing (yes, the I.R.S. labels me a "manufacturer") on a cus-

When applying maximum pressure on the rod, it doubles over into a "C". A "C-ing" rod not only demands the fish to exert maximum energy, shortening fighting time, but it also indicates to the crowd that you have a fish on.

43

tom built basis.

The first question I ask a prospective rod client is, "What weight line, or leader are you going to fish?" This illustrates just how important it is to fish with balanced spinning tackle. To select tackle which is out-of-balance will not only create nagging problems for you, but for those river rats who are fishing near you.

If you are a veteran steelheader you have witnessed the smooth operation of a crowd where others fish with balanced tackle. You have also "burned" when fishing with one who doesn't know the difference and messes up the smooth workings of the crowd. If you are about to make your first steelhead trip and feel the ultra-lite approach is more to your liking, the following details will help you avoid some of these pitfalls.

When choosing to fish ultra-lite, don't look for one of the common short ultra-lite rods. They are not long enough. However, they are designed to double over to cushion a particular weight line and this is the action you are looking for, but in a longer rod.

You do not want a short rod because it will not give you enough leverage when fighting one of these lunkers. A steelheader must maintain maximum pressure on the fish, in order to minimize fighting time and only longer rods (longer levers) offer you this extra effort.

For example: Tie a two pound line on a five foot rod designed for two and a 12 foot rod designed for two pound, then tie both lines to an object. Now, max both rods without breaking the line and feel the difference in the pressure you can apply. The law of physics, related to lever systems, makes this work and when fishing two pound test, you need all the help you can get.

Maximum pressure must also be exerted on the fish, because other near-by steelheaders will hold their rigs out of the water until you have the fish under enough control to land. You can only expect these sportsmen to wait for so long before they vent their feelings.

The longer rod will also give you greater line control during the drift. That is, it will allow you to hold more slack line out of the current. It is this slack line that creates a bow (belly) and the longer the cast, the more belly. Remember, the bait must remain at fish eye-level to get action, but a large bow will make this difficult to do. It will require you to add more weight to compensate and then this added weight can nag at you by hanging-up too often.

In 1972, when I made my first trip to Tippy Dam, I had replaced my Wonder Rod with a special order 10 1/2 foot fiberglass blank, designed by Gary Loomis at Lamiglas. Not only was this rod longer, it was designed to handle two-four pound test line, or leaders. It was the first "noodle" rod.

Upon arriving at Tippy, I was in awe of the massive dam and intimidated by its vast currents. Compared to the Elk and Betsie, this steelhead site was unbelievable.

Since I wasn't sure just how to get to Tippy, I came in well after daybreak and wasn't surprised to see steelheaders standing shoulder-to-shoulder. Like most newcomers, I stood far behind the line of casters, observing the procedures they practiced.

They were all fishing spin rods up to 8 feet long, because this was about the maximum length manufacturers were pumping out.

It's interesting how human nature takes over when fishing large water. Each time an angler cast, he'd unload like a shot-putter, firing the terminal rig as far as possible. "Farther" seemed to be "better!" Nevertheless, with everyone casting the same distance, at least it helped avoid tangled lines—to a certain extent anyway.

The big problem began when the rig landed and the current pulled the long slack line into a humongous belly. Surprisingly, a few anglers raised their rods high overhead,

Archie's early insight into drifting steelhead with a bobber has developed beyond his dreams.

sensing the need to reduce the bow in the line. Now, just how long can a person stand comfortably with an arm fully extended? They did what they could to reduce the bow, for as long as they could.

In addition to this type of compensating for an impossible situation, whenever a steelheader suspected a "take," he would back-pedal out of the water, to get slack out of the line, so he could set the hook. However, during his traveling time backwards, he not only placed his body in peril with the rock-strewn bank, but he would also be too late with the strike. The fish had already rejected the bait. While he would never really know if it was a fish, or bottom estate, being an avid steelheader, it was always a fish! "Oh Sh...!" became the universal cry during this time of disappointment. I have often threatened to write a book about the many similar final results I have witnessed over the past 33 years. Of course the book would have the fitting title, "Oh Sh...!"

As the morning progressed farther along than the fishing action, the normal attrition rate of anglers began. Having had the opportunity to "case" the water thoroughly, I soon had a

46

chance to slide in line with the others, as inconspicuously as anyone could toting a 10 1/2 foot rod.

Coming abreast the others, I began putting the final touches to my rig. During the interim, I could sense the stares and mumbling about the rod.

With confidence, I waited until my drift would merge with the others, then delivered the goods. At the first touch of bottom, I raised the rod straight up, pulling the slack line off the surface and out of the current, with my elbow resting at my side. A familiar hesitation in the drift caused me to lean the rod backwards and with a steelhead leaping, I announced to my new neighbors, "Fish on!" Within 45 minutes it was a threepeat.

It seems that regardless of where you fish, when you are successful, the "regulars" begin warming up by asking questions. These questions offered me the chance to not only answer the "how," but the opportunity to sell my rods.

Tippy Dam, became my new home base for steelhead. Within two years I was showing up at Tippy with 14 foot fiberglass rods, which offered more of an advantage. The walls of the rod blanks were super thin, making the rod truly ultra-lite in every way. They too were designed for two-four pound test mono. The term "whip" would have better described these noodle rods, as their soft action was better suited to two pound test. The many advantages of the longer rod quickly turned Tippy steelheaders to the noodle rods.

Another advantage was best demonstrated by Archie Sweet, who introduced bobber fishing to Michigan steelheaders. Since 1968, his home area at Tippy was just below the Coffer, where he drifted in the seams of the gushing currents, pouring over the structure.

Like the bottom bouncers drifting above the Coffer, Archie found it necessary to have absolute line control with the bobber. His problem was the same, slack line forming on the surface, which created a bow ahead of the bobber. With each indication of a fish, he had to first lift this bow off the surface before he could get the bobber off the water. By that time, the fish could have rejected the bait.

It was so critical, he always requested the longest rod I could conjure up. With the 14 footer held high, he removed every inch of slack from the surface. In fact, his direct contact to the bobber allowed him to bounce it once in a while, activating the bait. He never had to worry about missing fish again.

I witnessed this "accept and reject" mouthing habit of a steelhead in May of 1967, when fishing the Little Garlic River, in the U.P. I was sight fishing a male spawner and was wired to set the hook the second the spawn sac disappeared. As the sac was a hair away from its nose, it was suddenly some three inches back in front of him. I couldn't believe I missed the whole thing, it happened that quickly. I was a believer!

Archie's success with bobbers created a whole new ball game. The bobber opened up new waters for steelheaders to fish, waters too slow to bottom bounce. The bobber technique grew quickly, even crossing the border into Canada, where today Ontario steelheaders are float fishing with my noodle rods up to 18 feet.

During our 1977 summer trip to Washington, Gary Loomis and his brother Bob, spaced us out on the Kalama River and then the two of them took off to their own fishing spots. Archie was drifting his bobber along a nice long stretch of water for quite a while and was getting his share of action. He was on a drift when Gary and Bob returned over a rise. The minute Gary saw the bobber floating on the river, he began ribbing Archie with some rather choice words. When he was right in the middle of some highly colored phraseology, Archie's bobber disappeared, his rod came back and a silver missile soared skyward, instantly cutting off Gary's astute proclamation! Gary and Bob witnessed their "first."

Another advantage of fishing noodle rods is the ability to add pressure to the fish by pushing the butt cap forward until it is pointing at the fish, instead of fighting a fish in the usual manner, where the angler holds his forearm at 90 degrees. When a noodle rodder points the butt cap at his fish, the rod bends in the configuration of a big "C." It is this "Ceeing" rod the crowd wants to see, because it tells them you are putting maximum pressure on the fish, doing all that is possible to tire the fish. While this is just one of many techniques I developed with the noodle rod, it remains a very important one.

During those introductory days fishing at Tippy, another situation presented itself which was very bothersome to me. It occurred each time the fish neared the shore for beaching; it occurred because of the long searching leaders.

Each time a fish was ready to beach, I was adhering to the ol' fish-fighting adage, "Keep the rod up." However, with the rod held in a "Hi C," my split shot was hanging out of the water, swinging like a pendulum. I quickly pictured this pendular motion of the split shot working on the leader knot at the swivel and didn't like what I saw. So, I lowered the rod tip to the side, where the shot was in the water; where the water density would now cushion the working effect of the shot on the knot. "Low tipping" became a surer way of landing fish and this technique quickly caught on. Low tipping not only improved our landing success, but resulted in playing a more important role during the heat of battle.

One of the most wasted rod positions during the fight is

the traditional, "keep the rod up." The few times it benefits your efforts is when the fish is far downstream from you. A rod held high will show downstream anglers the approximate location of your fish, before you close the gap. A rod held high can also aid in avoiding bottom structures before you catch up to the fish. You want to close the gap with a downstream fighter as quickly as possible. This helps ensure the safety of the fish from anglers casting over your line.

Once you are abreast of the fish, forget the "Hi C," unless you eyeball threatening structures in front of you. Without such bottom obstacles, it is a waste of time and effort to apply lifting pressure to a bottom hugging trophy. Think of it this way: When maxing a rod held high, you are applying pressure in two directions, upwards and toward you. The pressure to pull the fish off the bottom is useless. The dead weight of the lunker allows it to lay there at rest, nullifying your energy to lift it. Again, try to pull 10 pounds of lead off the ground with your tackle.

What can you do when a fish decides to come to the surface in mid-stream? What does it gain you, aside from action shots with a camera? Unless you have a landing net with a very, very long handle, save this wasted energy and combine these two directions of applied pressure into one direction, by low tipping.

There isn't a more effective fighting maneuver than "low tipping" during the "close-in" fighting phase, for landing river lunkers from the bank.

Low tipping a middle-of-the-river bottom hugger, transfers maximum effort to pull the fish to shore. Now the fish must expend much more energy to keep from being pulled to you. Full lateral pressure will exhaust the fish faster, allowing those near-by anglers to get their rigs back into the river quicker. They deserve such consideration, as well as the fish.

Once the fish is brought to shore, the angler has a choice of netting, or beaching it. Netting fish in a current can be hazardous to the desired outcome and will require the rod to be held high in order to expedite getting the net under the fish. Beaching fish is, again, more effectively accomplished by low tipping.

I never carry a net, because even the best river rat can turn a fish-landing operation into a surface tennis match, with the fish winning. However, when I am guiding, I always carry a net, but for far different reasons than trying to net my client's fish. The net can become a bankside marker, designating "ownership" of this spot, as the client and I follow his fish downstream. It can also become the tote-bag for carrying fish clients want to keep.

My video cassette, "Chinook-Steelhead," vividly illustrates when to Hi-C and low tip steelhead. It also demonstrates the frustrations of netting these river dynamos compared to the ease of beaching them.

Now that I have established the noodle rod as the ultimate for those who love their ultra-lite fishing, there has been an interesting turn of events with rods which are designed for the real "meat" boys, in their pursuit for other

51

species of trophy fish. My first encounter with this type of meat stick came when Tom Janson got into jerking wire line for Lake Michigan lake trout, at the tiny port city of LeLand, Michigan. This was when Michigan-based Riviera began producing downriggers for our trolling fishery.

Janson's jerking gear consisted of a four foot "pool cue" with a large diameter wire reel mounted on it. The Monel wire line tested at 40 pound test and No. 5-6 Johnson spoons were the offerings. He would have to slowly spool out some 600 feet of wire to reach bottom where we trolled. Once on bottom, he vigorously pulled the rod back, then dropped the tip. It was jerk and drop, jerk and drop, until a fish was felt. Then it became one monotonous, long process of reeling in the fish. If the fish yanked too hard, it would tear loose from the hooks. This was when Tom asked if I could find a rod blank that had the backbone to set a hook, but just enough

I have just completed my 20th winter season on a 38-43 day sport show circuit.

give to prevent fish from tearing off. Herter's catalog helped me come to Janson's rescue.

While it was meat fishing, jerking wire was the most effective technique to take lake trout. Tom proved it by challenging a top-gun charter captain, who was already into trolling with downriggers. As usual, Janson humbled the captain—badly!

During the early 80s, I was exhibiting at a winter sport show in Arlington Heights, Illinois. Another custom rod builder, the late Joe Bonadon, came to my booth and asked me to come over to see a Musky rod he designed. It was also a four foot rod, but strung up with 50 pound mono. He had me turn slowly, wrapping the mono around both thighs. He shut down the drag on the reel, then told me to hold my ground while he tried to turn me back around with the rod. When the short rod bent into a C, it was all I could do to keep from getting turned around. It was really an eye-opener.

He wanted to show me even Musky fanatics don't have to fish with a pool cue. They can fish the same heavy line, but on a rod that will max into a Cee, during fighting time.

While exhibiting at Syracuse, New York, in the mid- 80s, a Shakespeare rep came to my booth and wanted to demonstrate some new rod concept which was just introduced to the East Coast, blue fin tuna buffs.

He first explained one problem with their traditional meat sticks, mounted with 150 pound test line. They were known to be the cause of producing back problems for anglers, sitting strapped in the fighting chair, getting jarred during the enduring fight.

He demonstrated the stiffness in the rod, then pulled another rod off the rack. He began telling me this Saber rod was designed on the West Coast and is the first to have enough give to prevent back ailments, yet handle 150 pound test. I believe it is this type of rod design that has brought on the recent "stand-up" fighting craze off our coasts.

When the Dipsy Diver (planer) came into our Great Lakes trolling fishery, 10 foot rods became the popular Dipsy rod. Its length helped keep the planer out-away from the side of the boat. The problem was, these rods were too stiff, causing a lot of break-offs and these Dipsys are not cheap. The quick cure was a "shock" cord, tied in-line ahead of the Dipsy. This shocker is doing the job for those who are stuck with these stiffer rods. However, though I don't troll with such tackle, I still build rods to sell. I found a great 10 foot blank that does it all for these guys, without the shocker and have moved quite a few.

The message of these few illustrations of rod design is the fact that power rods are not the answer to a heavy- duty angler's dream. Instead they have demonstrated their tendency to become a nightmare. If the rod can't bend below the first 12 inches from the tip, be prepared to lose as many fish as you land. I always like to include the following in my seminars: If you buy a rod that bends only halfway down the blank, I hope you bought it at half price. Too many rods are available now that will bend with any size line.

Surfin' Steelhead-Salmon
Chapter 6

I left Bullock Creek in the summer of '67 to take a football position at another brand new school district, Prairie Heights High School, in northeast Indiana. The move south meant a longer drive to my "honey" steelhead stream, the Elk River.

With the coming of Michigan's first fall runs of matured coho salmon, it also would mean a longer drive (after our Friday night games) to the Big Manistee River to see what these new fish were all about. As it turned out, they were awesome! The crowd was also awesome.

I fished below Bear Creek, where the crowd was so bad, a plane circled, broadcasting a warning to move our cars or get towed. What a joke! However, what wasn't a joke was when a Lake Michigan storm claimed the lives of seven trollers, who did not heed the warning of Coast Guard crews. It was the beginning of "coho fever." These coho caused me to return to Michigan the following summer.

A school superintendent I had met during my summer fly fishing jaunts to the South Branch of the Ausable River, offered me the Assistant Principal, Athletic Director and football coaching positions at yet another new school district in Jenison, Michigan. Needless to say, the combination of our usual spring steelhead and this fabulous new fall river fishery (coho averaging 14 pounds) found me eagerly moving back into Michigan in June.

Once settled in Jenison, I read a fishing report about a new Alaskan strain of coho salmon assaulting the Lake Michigan beach at Thompson Creek. This site is located just a long cast away from Manistique, in the U.P. I called a friend, John Pegram, about the news and we were on our way that weekend.

It was almost midnight when we arrived. We quickly slipped into our waders and vests, grabbed a spinning rod and headed down a path toward the beach. As we rounded the corner of some tall dense swale, we were greeted by a giant full moon appearing like a superball of red-hot lava.

While approaching the shore, we looked around to see the beach dotted with smoldering camp fires, rimmed with sleeping bodies. It took only one other glance to see we were the only ones intending to fish. Not sure just what to do first, we stood talking with eyes fixed on the smooth surface, looking for any disturbance on the water.

Suddenly, the surface boiled with a fish. I recovered my composure in time to get in the first cast. The spoon hit a few feet beyond the fading ripples. A short retrieve resulted in a wrist-jarring slam, triggering a shot of adrenaline searing through me. The surface instantly transformed into a series of miniature tidal waves. It became one grand display of super raw power, creating an exchange of some pretty strong expressions between John and me.

As pressure from the rod began sapping energy from the

I first read about the Thompson Creek runs of coho during Fourth of July, 1968. In just a few weeks this first salmonid surf site began taking on a dramatic high profile look.

prize fighter, it began to cruise the surface, defying pressure with its broadside tactics. As it continued to give ground, I was soon able to slip a hand over its broad neck. We were certain we would be able to take our limit of two fish during daylight, so I carefully released the gallant fighter.

When we hit the beach during the day, there unfolded another sight to behold. It was even more spectacular than the fiery moon. Before us stood a long line of waders, shoulder-to-shoulder some 30 yards out from shore. About 40 yards outside of them was a long line of car-top boats tied bow-to-stern. Both lines of anglers were fishing the slot of water between them, as swarms of coho ran the gauntlet. This scene was to become a weekly event.

Thompson Creek was not only unique in becoming the first surf site for salmonids anywhere, the coho themselves were unique. This Alaskan strain was ordained to come inshore in July, not in fall like the Oregon strain. However, because these Alaskan fish came inshore to run the rivers so early, they obviously didn't spend enough time feeding in the big water to attain the same size as the Oregon fish. Because they matured earlier, the Alaskan fish averaged six pounds, instead of the Oregon 14 pounders. Their July appearance also added a longer period of coho fishing for nontrollers.

I learned to bring my huge landing net, because it fast became my ticket to more gracefully merge among this jam-packed line of waders. I would simply stand back and offer my landing services to lucky anglers. One look at the size of the net erased all doubts of my ability to safely land their fish. After landing a couple of their coho, I became most welcome to join the party.

On one trip to Thompson, I brought along my two sons. Cole was entering 6th grade and Kurt, the 4th. Once I established my place in line, there was room for only one son at a time. When one would wade out in his bathing suit, we had to stand sideways, with me holding him tight against my stomach. It was because of this tight position that I invented the "hook cast" (as in the basketball hook shot).

Our first method for catching these coho was casting Dardevles. The gathering surfers served these spoons to the salmon on every imaginable type of rod and reel. Although there was this wide variety of tackle, all the anglers displayed one common practice. They all retrieved their spoons at the normal rate of speed. This resulted in sporadic success, but most did not seem to mind as they all seemed content being caught up in this new surf coho fever. However, having already spent several springs fishing river steelhead and enjoying hooking more fish than others, there had to be something I could do to conjure up more strikes from these marauding hordes of coho.

I had talked to several people who had trolled for fall coho. They said they had better luck with the (Oregon) coho by increasing the speed of their lures. I thought it was worth a try...and it worked! The faster retrieve made the difference! It was so successful I felt it deserved a special label, so I tagged it the "Thompson Creek Retrieve."

It got to the point where John and I would sit on the beach watching for fish to roll on the surface, behind the line of wading anglers. We took turns casting to the fish and with each cry, "Fish on!" the waders would turn around to watch our inside action.

News of this first surf site continued to spread like wildfire! Before the middle of August, license plates from Illinois, Wisconsin, Minnesota, Ohio, even Kansas, appeared in the new parking facility. Along with this growing horde of anglers came many different techniques. However, the bottom estate at Thompson Creek itself, called for a change of bottom fishing techniques, since bottom fishing with spawn began replacing spoons.

When the current of Thompson Creek flows straight out

into Lake Michigan, moss-covered rocks line the bottom on the south side of the current. Whenever we fished this side, the rocks gobbled up our terminal tackle. In contrast, the lake bottom on the north side of the current is pure sand.

It didn't take long for our Elk and Betsie river rats to begin showing up at Thompson Creek. It then turned into family outings, camping at local sites, including "Miami Beach," which was conveniently located on the beach next to the fishing site. Along with this gang of steelhead acquaintances came a pool of experience that would solve the problems of this bottom estate. In fact, before the mania at this surf site was over, eight of these steelheaders became my "field testers." They wore my Swan Custom Rods fishing vests to advertise my rods, which later would be tagged noodle rods!

Our first concern was how to fish more effectively on the rocky side of the creek. Ellis initiated the idea of floating spawn off the bottom with a piece of a party-size marshmallow. His recipe was to bite the marshmallow in half—you eat half and the fish gets half. Floating the bait above the rocks

It did not take long for "the boys" to begin their 300-400 mile hike to Thompson Creek, and by 1969 steelhead began swimming among the hordes of Alaskan coho which gathered at the mouth of the creek.

helped to eliminate at least one piece of terminal tackle from breaking off.

To keep the spawn from floating to the surface, Ellis pinched a small (BB) size split shot on the leader 6 to 8 inches from the hook. We referred to this technique as presenting the bait at "fish eye-level." It caught more fish than spawn lying on the bottom. Such success caused us to fish the same technique on the sandy side of the current. A plastic bag of party size marshmallows became something else to put in our fishing vest. When fishing was hot, it meant more half-servings for us to eat and when fishing was slow, the boredom meant eating more full sized ones. Either way, they could become bad for one's diet.

Along with this change in presenting bait, we also abandoned our use of three-way swivels. Instead, we opted for No. 10 barrel swivels and began experimenting with egg sinkers and bell sinkers, using them as a slip sinker. However, when these hung up they still cost us the entire terminal rig. This dilemma was solved by reverting back to our river drop-lines and split shot.

We slide one barrel swivel up the eight pound test main line and tie the drop-line to this barrel swivel. The split shot is pinched on the drop line. Now, the shot slips off the drop line when hung up, leaving us with only the shot to replace. It saves time out of water.

The eight pound test main line is tied to a second barrel swivel. This swivel becomes the stopper for the slip sinker, along with a three to four foot, four pound test leader tied to it. This terminal rig was so practical we continued to use it when fishing the sandy side of the creek. We also learned this slip sinker would remain far away from the leader during each scorching run, reducing leverage near the mouth of a head shaking fish.

It was surprising to find these coho chomping on food. After all, they were inshore preparing for their migration into the creek. We had already learned spawn run river steelhead were turned off to food, why not these coho?

Another thought-provoking situation began to unfold as steelhead started showing up amid the clouds of coho. Why would this big lake feeder move inshore with other fish? I always thought steelhead were solitary fish when feeding in

My wiggler bucket's other duties include raw coho spawn on a paper towel and airing party size marshmallows in its lid.

Ellis McColley became more interested in catching steelhead at Thompson where his new formula of offering more marshmallow than spawn, on a size 12 hook, proved to be the ticket.

the Great Lakes.

While the theories on these happenings were on my mind, there remained one unique fact—we were playing a role in establishing the first techniques to be used at other future surf sites.

With the growing chances of hooking steelhead, Ellis opted for these silver bullets over coho and began experimenting with different bait set ups. He was looking for something which might segregate the two fish. When he hit upon the combination of a smaller piece of spawn and a larger piece of marshmallow, he became encouraged at its results. As time passed, he proved this bait formula did separate steelhead from coho.

We also quickly learned that delivering food to these two fish in the clear still water of the lake, was as critical as presenting bait to steelhead in clear river water. Therefore, we continued to serve spawn and marshmallows on clear four pound test leaders and size 12, style 30, Eagle Claw wide bend hooks. I can best describe the logic of this surf prescription in the following manner:

Besides fishing with marshmallows, we also used them to locate the pooling creek water in the lake.

In a river, the fish maintains its holding pattern in the current, while you present the bait to the fish.

In the lake, the bait remains stationary off the bottom at fish eye-level; therefore, the fish presents itself to the bait. The fish has all the time in the world to cruise around looking the bait over. It better look appetizing. The clear, smaller diameter leader and small hook best serves this fillet mignon to a fish on a "silver platter."

During this time of using marshmallows, we learned they have a habit of dissolving in water. To help slow this process, we discovered exposing them to air forms a tougher skin. Then some coffee drinker got the idea to tear off a small piece of his styrofoam cup, substituting it for the marshmallow. This new combination continued to catch fish. However, while the fish didn't seem to mind the change of diet, we did. Ever try to eat a piece of styrofoam?

When the large numbers of coho and steelhead thinned down, so did the numbers of anglers. This made locating the fewer remaining fish more difficult, until we started to put it altogether.

The outflow of Harrisville's Mill Pond into Harrisville Harbor on Lake Huron, became our second surf site for steelhead.

It is the force and temperature of river water dumping into the lake that is the magnet drawing these fish inshore. In fall, river water will be cooler than the lake and these fish respond accordingly, because of their temperature sensitivity. This is important to remember when approaching any surf site in quest of feeders or pre-spawners.

This is so important, we first walked the beach to the mouth of the flow. To determine the direction the current was taking and how far, we tossed a few marshmallows into the flow. If it was a calm day, the current would flow straight out into the lake and the marshmallows would end up together

Like Thompson Creek, it didn't take long for steelhead to move in with returning coho salmon (Oregon strain) at the mouth of the Platte River, located in East Bay on Lake Michigan.

in a pool of water. If a strong wind caused the flow to bend along the shoreline, we wanted to know how close it ran to the shore and how far down the shore it went before fading out. Once all of this was determined, we made the necessary moves to cast to the target area.

When the lake was calm and the flow pooled, we targeted the pooling water. The larger the pool, the more fish would abound. The smaller pools made it necessary to fish the deepest edges of the current. This is important because fish are uneasy in clear, shallow water. They obviously seek out the deeper water for protection. They also opt to work in the edges of the current, where the broken water shields them from their enemies above.

When a wind turned the flow along the shore, we could spread out, expecting to find fish anywhere along the way. Whenever we had to face a wind, it made little difference where we fished, because the pounding surf negated the river flow.

Regardless of the wind direction, the dirty water created maximum security for the fish. Dirty water means fishing action will be enjoyed for a longer period.

In contrast, calm seas will offer abbreviated action. Knowing this finds die-hard surfers arriving before daybreak, since fishing action will usually be over when the sun hits the water. Cloudy days may prolong the action a little longer, but nothing beats dirty water conditions for surfin'.

Heavy surf at Thompson would also cause fish to wash up onto the beach, where they would immediately scoot back into the wash. Witnessing this, debunked the ol' salt tale that churning waters saturated with sand will cut into the gill filaments, killing the fish.

Landing fish in a heavy surf required special considerations also. We quickly learned to go with the flow. That is, we only pull on the fish when it is coming with a wave—never when it is in the backwash, or undertow!

Whether Thompson Creek was hot, or not, it was a weekend fishing trip, not a one day trip. As a result, Ellis opted to scout for a site closer to home. He found Harrisville Harbor on northern Lake Huron holding a few steelhead and spread the word among our Swan Rod group. He really got our attention when he beached an 18 pounder. This was the beginning of Harrisville becoming the world's second most viable salmonid surf site.

After the birth of Harrisville, the mouth of Platte River soon came on line. This surf site has proved to be the most "natural" of the three, due to stocking of what has become "Michigan" coho salmon. Since the first 1965 plant of coho, the Platte has received an annual average plant of over 1,000,000 fish.

Fishing success is contagious. The techniques we developed at Thompson are still successful today.

The King Of Salmon

Chapter 7

After enjoying the fantastic fall coho fishing on the Big Manistee River, my first football season at Jenison was a good reason for fishing closer to home. This, plus the fact that our first fall run of Chinook salmon would be coming into the Muskegon River, just a long cast away. This run of fish was composed of jacks, which is a fish that sexually matures one year ahead of its normal four year cycle. These three year olds were averaging the same weight as the coho, 12 to 14 pounds.

My target site for these kings was the popular Newaygo Dam located at Newaygo, Michigan. It was more of a spill-way, instead of a barrier dam, one which many of the leaping chinook could clear. This would allow these leapers to continue upstream to the true barrier, Croton Dam.

Believe me, when I say popular, I mean anglers packed into a small productive piece of water and spectators jammed in on top of us. It was more of a spectacle than a fishing experience, but having the years of crowd fishing already under my belt, I wasn't about to miss out on this new fish.

With all due respect to this juvenile king-of-them-all, they didn't show me anything more than the coho. They required the same need for us to bounce bottom, they did not jump when hooked and showed the same fighting tactics, but they were chinook, Lake Michigan's first king salmon.

The next fall, our first return of adult kings was unbelievable! They were everything they were touted to be...and then some. Like others, I was armed with heavy artillery. I had put together a rod that would "C" with 30 pound test. Yes, the ol' lite-liner himself opted for "cable." It was a blast! However, the time came when everyone was doing the same thing and it fell into a routine. There had to be another site, another approach for these blockbusters.

By this time the Michigan Fish Division had already diluted the Alaskan coho gene pool, discouraging me to take the long drive to Thompson Creek. Not being a troller, this time of year became a bummer, a void that needed filling. I still could not get myself to return for those Hex hatches on the South Branch of the Ausable. I was spoiled with "lunker fever." After hooking and landing steelhead, coho and chinook, I was afraid I would yank a stream trout out of the water when setting the hook.

It wasn't until I was seated in the local barber's chair that I was offered hope for getting into some fish. Dale VanderLaan was the most fish crazy barber I had ever met and when he offered me a fishing trip for chinook, I eagerly accepted. Being a river rat, I thought it would be a nice change of pace to jump into a big boat and do some trolling.

Dale pulled up to my house at 3:30 a.m. and I thought I was still asleep as my eyes fell upon the 14 foot boat, sitting on a trailer. I made no comment, but my mind was whirling as we headed north to the port city of Manistee. I didn't say a word either, as he turned east off of U.S. 31, instead of west, to Lake Michigan.

Taking back roads eastbound, then heading north, we came rolling down a long hill with a lake sitting at the bot-

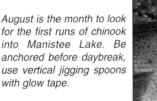

August is the month to look for the first runs of chinook into Manistee Lake. Be anchored before daybreak, use vertical jigging spoons with glow tape.

August is the time of year when chilled nights react to the warm lake water temperatures creating fog. Over the years, fog has proven to create the best chinook action.

tom. It was East Lake, the eastern-most body of water in the Manistee Lake complex.

We unloaded the boat at the public ramp in Stronach. There were others unloading, so I was a little more sure he knew what he was doing. He rowed out about 40 yards and had me drop the anchor.

"Rig your gear just like you do for steelhead," came my first instructions. I quickly inquired, "You're kidding— swivels, spawn bag and all?" "Yep!" Dale replied, "and toss it as far as you can, let it settle to the bottom, then hold onto your rod...tight."

As I sat waiting for action, with my rod cradled across my legs, I began to survey this small body of water still loading up with boaters. Suddenly, I felt the rod handle lifting off my legs and at the same time, watched the rod tip bending under the boat. I quickly swung the long rod around the bow

69

of the boat, then came back hard on it. The drag started screeching at a steady pace. It felt as though I was hooked to a trolling boat instead of a fish. The fish finally stopped and began shaking its head violently, with the rod tip bucking hard with each thrashing movement. Suddenly my rod snapped back in the air and the line hung limp. My fish was gone!

This was my introduction to this unique chinook salmon fishery—a small lake fishery that I have annually taken part in and one that continues to be a challenge.

Leaving Jenison and moving up to Clare has put me closer to my river fishing and also closer to this early chinook fishery. The fishing on East Lake hasn't changed through the years, but some new methods have developed, along with a very noticeable change of attitude among the fishermen.

On one of my earlier trips, I had my two daughters with me. Jaymie, at 14, was seated midship, Jill, 9, was up front, and I was seated in the back of a rented 12 foot boat. With three rods poised, Jill's started to move into a slow arching position. Jaymie and I took the clue and reeled our lines in to avoid entangling Jill's. Jaymie leaned toward Jill to make sure she was doing everything right, when the fish took its first marathon run.

I quickly tossed our marker bottle overboard and started rowing in pursuit of the fish. Jill had a good grip on the 10 foot rod as the tip pointed the direction I should follow. The bending rod also showed other fishermen the path the fish was taking and they obligingly lifted their anchors as we moved along. The strain on Jill's face brought smiles and encouraging words from nearby fishermen.

As the fish slowed and I closed the gap, I sensed we would soon have a chinook. The close-in tactics of these tugging brutes are usually predictable. They will swim around the boat a few times, come under the boat, surface, head deep again, come up on their side and into the net. This was Jill's first trip, so she wasn't familiar with their fighting routine.

As the fish came toward the boat, Jill's rod tip suddenly pointed a new direction the fish was taking—straight down! Jaymie was still giving Jill her full attention as she began pumping the fish upward. The salmon hit the surface, saw the boat, and bored straight down to the bottom. The bending rod tip splashed into the water and the force of the raising rod butt pulled Jill up off her seat. Jaymie made an instinctive arm-wrapping tackle around Jill's waist.

Since Jill had now become the center of attention, this surprising move by both girls drew laughter from the other fishermen. The fish was pulled to the surface, where I eased the big net under the 26 pound lunker. The lake came alive with air horns blasting, hands clapping, and loud cheers.

That type of response from other fishermen was common back in those earlier days, but this kind of camaraderie has long since faded. Now, there is a far less personable atmosphere hanging over this tiny fishery. This change of attitude, along with a desire to change the technique of catching these monsters, caused me to take a new look at this fishery. I had some ideas in mind and was eager to try them out.

In order to apply light line to these East Lake chinook, I knew I would have to be rid of neighboring anchor ropes. I talked to Tom Janson about this idea of catching chinook on tournament two pound test. Since Tom was a two- time world record holder for steelhead caught on two pound test, it wasn't surprising when he eagerly responded, "When do you want to go?"

I also talked about another method of fishing these chinook, one that was completely foreign to Tom and me. We agreed that we would have to take the gamble by driving to East Lake at such an early date that few boats would be on the lake. This meant, although we might reduce the number of boats present, we could also be fishing in a lake with no chinook. We chose August fifth as a time to begin experimenting.

The anchor that Tom dropped was at the mouth of the Little Manistee River and off the shallow shelf in 18 feet of water. We chose this location because of the instinct salmon have for returning to their parent stream. We also knew the river current would carry colder water into the warmer lake, so we would have two factors working for us in attracting any early salmon to this area. The third advantage going for us was the deeper structure. Colder water should be located near the bottom at this time of year, and if there was such a thing as salmon being guided by bottom structure, we were anchored on "home base."

We impaled nightcrawlers through the tips of their nose with our No. 12 hooks, injected a small bubble of air into their tails, tossing them as far as our long whips could cast them. We sat back, ready for action. Our topic of conversation was the strange feeling of being on East Lake completely alone! This was better than we anticipated. All we could hope for now was that some chinook had taken the crazy notion to leave Lake Michigan and head into East Lake. There was no surface action to show the big brutes were in and after an hour and a half, boredom was setting in. I then decided it was time to go into Phase II of this fishing trip.

I had brought along my 10 foot meat stick with an open-face reel loaded with six pound test mono. I had also brought along one spoon to fish. I lowered the spoon to the bottom of the lake. With the rod tip on the surface, I reeled the spoon up about six inches. I then made a motion with the rod that was new for me. I began jigging—vertical fishing! A quick sharp lift on the flexible rod shot the spoon up about three feet upward. I immediately dropped the rod tip to the surface, allowing the light metal spoon to flutter back down to its starting point.

In less than five minutes, while raising the rod, the tip suddenly remained glued to the surface. As the rod developed into the big "C," Tom reeled up both of our other rigs. During this time, the fish chose to swim around in a short circle, occasionally shaking its head. "It's probably a pike," I muttered.

Then, as if reacting to a starter's pistol, the fish sprinted across the lake. We laughed as the line peeled off the spool. There was no question in our minds as to what species I was hooked into. With the spool carrying 400 yards of mono and no other boats to worry about, we remained at anchor while this long distance skirmish continued. I finally worked the fish back to the boat and Tom slipped the net under a gallant, 24 pound chrome-plated king salmon.

I handed the rod to Tom and said, "Here, it's your turn." He wasn't long in bringing our second salmon to net and by 10:30 a.m., we had three beautiful chinook.

Our long lines proved to be a waste of time while the jigging spoon got the job done. Its dramatic success provided us

In August of 1980, I added a new twist to the Manistee Lake chinook program, with the Lite Liner *serving as the "mother ship" and Jim's pram as the chaser.*

a philosophical session during our drive home. It was one which, over the years, seems to be a fact of a chinook's life.

When these early silver fish decide to leave Lake Michigan to enter Manistee Lake, they represent a different stage of their four-year life cycle, a stage that had gone undetected by inland fishermen. For lack of a better term, I refer to this as the "in-between" stage.

These early run fish are as silver as those still on the feed in Lake Michigan, only these are not feeders. These early migrators have not yet taken on any visible pre- spawning, physiological changes. There is no change in the jaw structure of the male king, therefore, it is still difficult to guess their sex.

Since there is no change in the jaw formation, fishermen with long lines sitting on the lake bottom are wasting their time. Bottom fishing only pays off after their upper jaw begins to hook. In contrast, when the jaws do begin to take on this secondary characteristic, these fish show very little interest in our jigging spoons.

74

When trollers are blown off the big lake, some sneak into East Lake, where we notice the percentage of hook-ups lean heavily toward those of us who are jigging. I believe this noticeable difference is because the fish is not interested enough in feeding to chase fast-trolled lures.

It seems a lure that is jigged in a vertical motion can become more irritating to a nonfeeding chinook. A lure that moves only a few feet, does not require a great desire to chase. The rhythmic jigging motion lends itself more to irritating fish, or to conveniently time his crunch on the descending spoon. We have been proving this by having never hooked a fish once the spoon was on its way up. The heavy fish is felt the instant we lift the rod.

The warmer water temperatures of East Lake cause the chinook's spawning characteristics to develop at a rapid rate. So, our success in jigging for these fresh fish has been limited to one or two weeks. As Labor Day nears, there is a noticeable increase in boats and a noticeable change in the features of the fish. It is at this time that I leave the lake, put on my waders, and begin fishing in the manner I enjoy most—river fishing.

Michigan's Lower Peninsula offers small boat fishermen many sheltered waters in which to fish chinook: Muskegon Lake at Muskegon, White Lake at Whitehall, Pentwater Lake at Pentwater, Pere Marquette Lake at Ludington, Manistee Lake (East Lake) at Manistee, Boat Harbor at Leland, Lake Charlevoix (mouth of Jordan and Boyne Rivers) at Charlevoix (or Boyne City), Boat Harbor at Harrisville (Lake Huron), and the water discharge at Harbor Beach (Thumb area).

At many of these sites, few will be attempting small boat fishing. That is, until they see your big landing net go over the side and capture a prize chinook salmon. From mid-August through September, car top fishermen can get into the king of them all.

Trolling Chinook Salmon... the Sporting Way

Chapter 8

The long rod slammed hard over the stern of the boat, with each graphite fiber straining to keep the stretching rod intact! The big bait reel was shedding monofilament from its spool at an unbelievable rate of speed. In order to remove the laid-out rod from its holder, my wife quickly reached for the star drag to loosen it. Once removed, she tucked the rod butt in her stomach and pulled the 12 1/2 foot noodle rod back over her shoulder. By this time I had slipped the gas lever to neutral and had both electric downriggers on their way up. I soon cleared the other rod from the water.

As the fish continued to melt line, there was no question about it, this screamer was a chinook. When it collided with the No. 5 J-Plug, it never slowed down...until it finally surfaced some 60 yards away. Like all the others, it too began to cruise along the surface, like a miniature Jaws, with its dorsal and top of its tail out of the water. What a great picture, seeing this stubborn brute broadsiding us in the dead-calm sea.

The unrelenting pressure on the rod soon turned the head of the chinook. This was the first sign of it tiring and it soon began giving up yardage. As it neared the boat, it slowly swam down under the boat. At this, Chuck buried the rod in the water, allowing the line to clear the out-drive. Clearing the prop, she raised the rod slowly, making sure to clear the four foot downrigger arm, then shuffled to the other side of the boat to put the finishing touches on the 18 pound spring chromer.

We were trolling on Lake Michigan, out of the port of Ludington, in June of '82. It was a most unusual month, as

the chinook remained on a feeding frenzy in water temperatures in the 40s, down to 22 feet deep.

The constant cold water temperature was not the only unusual happening on Lake Michigan. For the first time since the birth of this Great Lakes trolling fishery, I would run a charter service trolling two to eight pound test mono on downriggers. This was the beginning of a personal endeavor to prove the biggest salmon in the Great Lakes can be caught in a more sporting manner. I would begin chartering for chinook in August.

This was the culmination of a dream which began in the summer of '65, after trolling for coho salmon out of Coos Bay, Oregon. Since we would receive our first run of immature coho in the fall, I thought it would be a good idea to first learn what I could about these fish from the West Coast "pro's."

It was the experience of having the first mate crank the drag down tight on my reel, so I would have to crank the fish faster, that turned me off. That style of man-handling fish was not for me. However, it would later become the same method of trolling adopted by Great Lakes charter captains.

Before I go into detail about my lite-lining practices, I want to take these traditional trolling methods and put them in their proper perspective. I want you to see if you recognize yourself in the following scenario:

You are a babe-in-the-woods when it comes to trolling on the Great Lakes. Your bag has been challenging the local bass, pike, walleye and enjoying it. However, your buddies keep harping at you to join them on their next charter trip for chinook. They stay on your back to where, in spite of your being a very independent thinker, you finally yield. After all, chinook average slightly over 15 pounds and from what they say they are mean-machines, a cut above the species you are into. It will only cost you $80 for several hours of fishing and brotherhood.

As you walk along the docks looking for your boat, the "meat wagon," you are in awe of the size of these "Charter Row" boats. I swear, the rationale for charter captains having such large boats lends itself to—the higher the bridge on the boat, the closer to godliness!

You are soon greeted by Captain Ahab, with his eyes rolling up like a cash register, as the six of you step aboard. Ye ol' matey points out your choice of seating and off you go into the wild blue yonder.

With all 16 rods set doubled over in the rod holders (Michigan allows two rods per angler), being polite, you don't mention how the boat now reminds you of the back end of a porcupine. However, if you were on a charter trip in Indiana (where three rods per angler is the law), the boat would look like the back end of a porcupine in heat!

Suddenly, you see ye ol' matey lunge toward a rod. He quickly removes it from the rod holder, then in a backbreaking motion, he whams the hook home...once...twice...three times. Such jaw-jarring rod sets cause flashbacks to your Saturday morning T.V. screen, featuring the good ol' boys attempting to behead those poor 1 1/2 pound bass, with a

cue stick and 17 pound test cable.

Ye ol' matey then turns, looks at you and with bowing grace, beckons you to the rod. You approach to where ye matey firmly plants the rod butt into your midsection, then with authority, instructs you to, "Start reeling!"

Being a respectful person, you do as instructed. In a short time, the idea of standing there cranking on the reel finally hits home and you begin to question if your monotonous reeling is anything more than becoming a human winch.

Phase II of this trolling experience begins as your fish finally nears the boat. It starts when ye matey reaches for the landing net. Unfortunately, manufacturers just don't make them with handles long enough. As a result, you hear an added command, "Back up and keep reeling!" Now at least you become a moving robot. While moving backwards, you see your buddies watching the netting action. Ye matey makes a stab with the net. You know he missed because you are ordered to, "Keep backing up and reel faster!" When your rod hits the bridge, where Captain Ahab resides at the wheel, you have a panoramic view of the activity going on at the stern. Finally, a roar goes up from your pals. Through somewhat glazed eyeballs, you see the netted fish come winging over the transom and into "the box."

Your buddies swarm on you with shoulder slaps, high fives and low-fives. Now you are able to approach the open coffin to finally get a look at your fish. While looking, you feel your intellect returning, your self-respect resurfacing and immediately, you do some soul-searching:

"Just what was this all about? Did I miss something in all

of this? Did I really enjoy this?" Then finally, "I paid $80 for this?"

Well now Babe-in-the-woods, if you think that experience was something, just be happy you didn't lose the fish! Talk about some real verbal abuse...and for $80.

No, this event does not depict all charter operators, but it does occur far too often.

After my Coos Bay trolling experience and hearing stories about the same approach used by Great Lakes captains, I was convinced there had to be a way to change this trolling routine. The adjustments I came up with are relatively simple.

Monofilament: I had talked to others who attempted to troll four pound test, but they expressed problems with it breaking at the release on the cannonball. When I asked the brand of line they used, no one mentioned Berkley XT. When it comes to two pound test, none can compare to clear colored XT. Without it, it would be impossible for me to troll No. 5 J- Plugs 90 feet down, on two pound test.

Releases: A troller can go nuts trying to select one of the many releases available. Along with the variety of models comes the range of prices. None filled the bill for me. Instead of these, I opted for one which had been around for a few years. It was the rubberband! For me, it was the No. 16 rubberband.

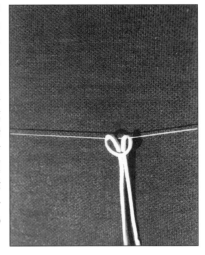

It has been flawless, with the thin mono cutting through it like butter. It's rare to have a false release off my giant paper clip, which I attach to the ball. How's that for coming up with something functional—and so cheap?

Downriggers-

Every morning, I begin a trolling program setting only two rods, with one lure on each. I will only add one, or two other rods if the fishing action is absolutely dead, which is unusual.

When Canon first marketed the Digi-Troll, I installed two of them. Each of these are programmed to lift and lower a cannonball five feet. This enables me to set one cannonball, say, at 27 feet, then punch the 15 second mode. This lifts the ball (bait) five feet up (to 22 feet) in 15 seconds, then lowers it back down to 27 feet in 15 seconds. It continually covers these depths of water at 15 second intervals, until re-programmed. The second cannonball is lowered to 17 feet, five feet above the 22 foot depth of the other ball, then programmed to lift (to 12 feet) and lower every 15 seconds. The two lures cover 15 feet of water every 15 seconds. It takes three other riggers to cover the same depths.

When Canon introduced the Digi-Troll II, I picked one up to replace an original 'Troll, which went bad. The 'Troll II allows a depth selection of 17 feet. Programming 17 feet on the new one and the five feet built into the old 'Troll, has two lures covering 27 feet. Without two Digi-Trolls, it requires approximately five downriggers to cover these same depths.

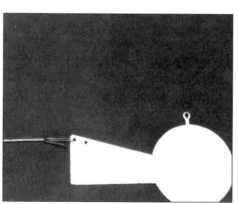

Most marketed downrigger releases are of the gator-clip variety, where the clip is squeezed open and the line is placed between the two padded ends.

During a three day period of chartering with only one (the other needed repair), the 'Troll registered 57 hits, while the other scored one!

Reels: Some trollers blame their reels for not being able to use light line. It's no wonder, because the most popular reels were too big to have a drag which could be fine-tuned to handle the lighter weight mono.

My 1981 summer steelhead trip to Washington, convinced me of which reels to troll with. There are no steelheaders anywhere else who rely more on quality bait reels than West Coast river rats. I saw more Shimano Bantam reels than any other brand. I wanted the largest capacity Bantam with a drag system smooth enough to handle my two and four pound lines. Their biggest, the Bantam 500, filled the bill. It holds over 1,000 yards of two and four pound test, with a drag light enough to create a backlash if loosened all the way. In today's market, there are several companies with level wind reels which fill this bill.

The purpose for the deep spool was to cut out refilling the spool during a day of trolling, whether it was necessary because of break-offs, or simply breaking off line which was abraided.

Rods: Because the noodle rods were specifically designed for this weight line (not leaders, since I troll with straight line off the reel), they obviously adorned the rod holders aboard the Lite Liner. However, once the Bantam was mounted on the noodle rod, like all other poorly manufactured trolling rods, the rod bent over backwards when under stress. This forces the line to pass below the shaft of the bending rod, often times rubbing against the rod. I certainly did not need that happening, especially with such light monofilament.

The solution came fast and easy. I immediately pictured my brother's innovative off-to-the-side stripper guide. This slight adjustment of guides on the butt section of the rod corrected the problem. Since I borrowed the idea from Jay, I thought it only fitting to keep it in the family. I call it the Swan Twist!

With a trolling reel mounted on top of the rod, I wrapped the first butt guide on top of the rod. This picked up the line off the reel in the usual fashion. My second guide, however, was cocked to the side of the rod, so its large ring was slightly under the rod. This pulled the line from the top guide out-and-around the rod. The third and final butt guide was wrapped on the bottom of the rod, completing the twisting path of the line. The top section of the rod is then ferruled with its guides in line with the bottom butt guide.

The fact that Fenwick was not interested in the Swan Twist, and Eagle Claw tried, but never followed through with it, bears out how tradition too often stifles invention.

You remember my mentioning how steelheaders at Tippy felt the need to do something to compensate for their short rods, so they held them high in the air? Well, many trollers don't like to see their rods bending backwards in the rod

holders, so they turn the rods over with the reel and guides facing down. While this prevents the less desired backward look while trolling, the minute a fish is hooked, the rod has to be turned up again during fighting time.

The fact is, if the Swan Twist was incorporated on all trolling rods, boaters could then fish a much more functional rod.

Hooks: Most top fish-producing trolling lures come from the manufacturer with inferior hooks installed. These are impractical to use because they will not hold a point. Veteran trollers discard them, opting for their own favorite hooks. Fishing with light line, I had still another concern.

My number one trolling lure is the No. 4 and 5 J-Plug, but I must tie my own harnesses. For this and all other alterations, I used to buy Eagle Claw, style 375 treble hooks in sizes 1 through 8. More recently, I have switched to VMC's round bend in the same sizes. They are thinner wire hooks, serving a sharper point. Mepps makes a dangerous hook. It is so sharp, it seems to draw skin to it like a magnet. It does a great job penetrating jaws too.

Boat Handling: It makes no difference what size boat is used to catch lunkers on light tackle; the maneuvering requirements are generally the same. The first boat handling requirement is to stop the boat the second a fish is hooked. After immediately gathering in the other rods and cannonballs, the lucky angler can now enjoy the full power of each fish, without having the boat drag the fish around the lake.

With the boat dead in the water, the angler actually gets to "pump-and-reel" the fish all the way to the net. This is almost impossible to do when dragging fish with the boat, because the momentum of the boat takes away the slack

needed to be able to reel after the pump.

I look at it this way: Most of us come from the inland lake, warm water fishery. We cut our teeth on bass, perch, bluegills and pike, while fishing from car top boats. Can you remember the time when you quietly worked the boat into range of a favorite casting lane near lily-pads? Do you remember when the top water bait was viciously slammed by a mean mouth bass...and you immediately revved up the motor, dragging the bass out of the pads? I hear you laughing, but yet you do it when you troll in a large snag-free lake.

Great Lakes trollers will never know just what each species of fish is capable of doing when on the other end of the rod. Aboard the Lite Liner we have lake trout which will go under the boat two or three times, before coming to the net. Yes, even the lowly ("greaser") lake trout has a bag of tricks it loves to pull on you if given the chance. If the laker can fight this much, just think what coho, chinook and steelhead can do. Wow!

I already mentioned that the most common rod maneuver is to bury the rod in the lake when fish dive under the boat. This is another advantage of trolling longer rods. There is little chance of the line scraping the bottom of the hull, or getting into the motor's prop. However, if it does get caught in the prop, there is still a chance of getting the line free, if the boat is not moving. There has not been one day on the lake that I don't hear a radio report telling of a fish that got into some troller's downrigger cables, shutting the boat down for up to an hour.

I doubt if other trollers experience fish who come to the boat, then "sound," defying you to lift it. If it had not been for my East Lake experiences with chinook, I would have been out of luck when they sound in the depths of Lake Michigan. However, on East Lake, it only required me to tow (by rowing slowly) the sounder into the shallows, where it was easy to net. With the shallow shoreline too far to tow a Lake Michigan sounder, I improvised a similar move in the deeper lake.

When it is determined the sounder cannot be lifted, I free-spool the reel, taking all pressure off the fish ("loose-line" the fish), then slide the boat into gear and slowly move away from the fish. You must loose-line the fish, because any pressure on the fish will cause it to come right along with you, like a dog on a leash.

With no other boats around, move your boat 40 to 50 yards away from the fish, then shut down. Lock up the spool and come back on the rod. The angle of the pull will now allow you to bring the fish to the surface. This angle is the

Jerry Gibbs, Fishing Editor, Outdoor Life, went five for five, with chinook up to 23 pounds, on two pound test mono while trolling out of the port of Ludington.

only thing that will pull the fish to the surface. It is impossible to lift the dead weight of a sounder! Not so? Well, take your meat rod and cable, tie it to a 10 pound weight. Now lift it off the floor. Case closed!

Think about it. The reason a fish does not sound on the average troller, is because the continued moving of the boat maintains this same angle.

When I first chartered for fall chinook, I ran 8 to 10 pound test tackle. My clients landed 100 percent of their hook-ups, unless the fish was cut-off by another boat, or the hook pulled loose. In my opinion, whenever a trophy becomes a guaranteed catch, it is time to change the rules of the game. When the challenge of fishing is removed, stick with perch, or bluegills. As a result, I removed this tackle from the Lite Liner, opting for only two, four, and six pound tackle. Since then, the six pound line averages a 95 percent landing success. It is this five percent chance of losing the fish which keeps clients from getting too cocky, or too bored while the rod is bending. The four pound test drops the landing rate to 75 percent and the two pound test, to 65 percent.

To those who do not troll on the Great Lakes, these averages might not mean much. However, when you know that the president of the Michigan Charter Boat Association went on public record writing, "We run a taxi service for unskilled fishermen boating half the fish they get on a hook," it illustrates how many more fish would be landed if the boat was shut down during fighting time.

Since 1986, our chinook fishery in Lake Michigan has gone to hell in a hand bag. The dilemma is the out-break of Bacterial Kidney Disease (BKD). Oddly enough, it is only chinook that die from this malady, even though all other salmonid stocks show positive clinical symptoms of BKD.

BKD has had a very dramatic impact on Lake Michigan chinook stocks! How dramatic is it? Well, our 1986 annual creel census shows a high of 382,033 chinook boxed. Our

1993 creel census was 27,284!

With this Lake Michigan chinook problem and charter captains who continue landing one half of their hooked fish, the Lite Liner continues to maintain its unbelievable average of boated fish.

The first part of my two-part fishing video, "chinook-Steelhead," features two young girls, 11 and 15 years old, boating 10 of 10 hooked chinook. If you have a problem believing what you read here, you can see it!

Super Skamania Steelhead

A s my fly moved slowly through the deep hole, I noticed a telltale hesitation in the drift. This triggered a reflex response with the long rod, a response which caused all hell to break loose as the river exploded with steelhead!

One silver torpedo erupted from the river performing a series of horizontal jackknifes, while another reached up six feet, stared us in the eye, then performed a "dead fall" entry back into the river. Another chrome-slabbed monster sought refuge in the branches of an overhanging tree, five feet above the surface, while yet another violently threw itself sideways out of the water, crashing its silver armor- plating against the protruding root of a tree!

It was an awesome display of raw power generated in the musculature of this particular strain of steelhead. It was a fireworks spectacular I had never witnessed in all my decades on steelhead rivers. I would never know which of the four star performers took the fly. It really didn't matter, as we stood numbed by the sky-filled superstars. It was a steelheader's dream come true, as I continued to hook 50 to 60 more of the river beasts, landing only one "small" 13 pounder. My arms and fingers cramped to where I could no longer cast, or tie terminal rigs. Every steelheader should experience such agonizing bliss!

On the 4th of July, we were

For Jim Grzywinski of Toledo, Ohio, it was a lucky Fourth of July as he boated this 17 pound 10 ounce world record steelhead on IGFA 2 pound test.

trolling on Lake Michigan. The lake was dead calm and the sun was broiling us at 94 degrees. I had two red Hot-N-Tots, one 60 feet behind the cannonball, down 22 feet and the other the same distance back and 27 feet down. We were just about to shut the Lite Liner down, haul in the tackle and take a plunge into the lake when a silver missile turned the calm blue surface into a frothing tsunami!

No one moved while this chromer hung poised before our eyes, not 10 feet from the downrigger arm. It was as though we were transfixed by the grandeur of this spectacle. In reality, however, no one moved because neither of the rods had moved. They remained in their trolling position. Once back in the water, however, it was Katy bar-the-door as the 13 foot rod slammed so far over the boat's transom, its tip pierced the surface.

As line disappeared from the big Bantam reel, it quickly formed a maze on the surface. A third explosion by the fish was 30 yards and 90 degrees from its second leap and a fourth was back in the area of its second. The speed of this greyhound was such that the line could be seen at each of its entry sites! I was reeling line coming back in a zig-zag pattern. Its speed defied description!

This type of trolling action took place several times a day over a four to six week period, in June and July, while chartering in this area of Lake Michigan.

These two steelhead dream sites were not found in Michigan waters. This wonderland of super steelhead was located in Indiana, but was finally on its way to Michigan, Illinois, Wisconsin, other Great Lakes states and Ontario.

In 1985, during my eight summers chartering in Indiana, I hosted the defensive unit of the Dallas Cowboys. This was "America's Team" with "Too Tall" Jones, John Dutton, Randy White and Jim Jeffcoat, along with the Defensive Coordinator, Ernie Stautner. Now let me tell you, there is no way in hell any single boat could handle such a combined mass of human protoplasm. I had to put out an S.O.S. and my good friends, Mike McKee, out of Michigan City, and Flint's Dave Arff, out of Burnham Harbor in Chicago, Steve Lanford came to my rescue. This was to be a two-day video shoot for what finally turned out to be an aborted attempt to land me a T.V. series, "Trophy Fishing."

With the camera on my boat, I received a call on our private radio channel from Mike:

"Hey Dick, Jeffcoat's got a leaper on!" At this, we hauled in the two rods and were on our way.

As we carefully rounded the stern of Mike's Starcraft One, the big camera was rolling in time to record Jim's steelhead firing out of the lake. The silver missile was on a dead-on course to

The Barrier Dam on the Cowlitz River was our most consistent fishery during the four summer visits to Washington.

torpedo Jim directly in the chest. However, its trajectory was slightly off course, causing it to slam into Mike's starboard side!

The impact of the silver iron-side's collision with aluminum, catapulted it back into the water some six feet away, where it immediately soared skyward again, firing the orange J-11 Rapala back at Jeffcoat. After listening to Jim's instant replay, over and over, he could still be trying to get even with that worthy "opponent" every Sunday afternoon.

This steelhead strain was developed in the state of Washington, at the Skamania Hatchery in 1956. It is a genetic strain designed to enter rivers during summer months. While it is a spawn-run fish at this time of year, it doesn't spawn until late January into February.

In the late 70s, Indiana was looking for a steelhead stock different from what was already swimming in Lake Michigan. Indiana's biologists looked to Washington's summer strain, liked what they saw and have been rewriting steelhead history ever since.

West Coast steelheaders call this fish a summer steelhead, while the Hoosiers enthusiastically tag it a Skamania. Whichever name you choose to call it, it is spelled, s-u-p-e-r s-t-e-e-l-h-e-a-d!

In 1977, I made my first summer trip to Washington to fish these fabled fighters. The trip came about as a result of Jerry Gibbs, outdoor editor with Outdoor Life asking me if I thought the long rod, lite line technique would be as successful on Washington rivers. His question got the wheels moving.

I contacted the builder of my rod blanks, Gary Loomis. There can't be a more intense West Coast steelheader than Gary. He assured me there would be summer fish available in June and July. He also mentioned their fish would certainly put our technique to the test. From his reports, I knew we would be fishing when the coastal rivers would be in critical condition, low and clear. It is the same river condition that exists in Michigan most of the year.

As June 6 neared, the phone to Washington was hot. We arranged for a Winnebago motor home to pick up on our way through Iowa. This would be home for me and three of the Swan Rod team. The group included Archie Sweet, Mike VerBerkmoes and Burl Brown. Tom Janson would drive out with freelance writer Steve Griffin, who would cover the trip for a magazine. After Kurt's June 6th high school graduation

Bob Koch, Indiana's former chief biologist for Lake Michigan, managed to land a hellion during my invitational trip to the Little Calumet River.

exercise, the four of us jumped into my big wagon and headed west.

Our hosts and guides were members of the South King County (T.U.) Steelhead Chapter. They led us by the hand as we fished the Green, Cowlitz, North and South Forks of the Toutle and Kalama rivers. We concluded the three week tour logging 131 fishing hours and fought 121 of the raucous demons. It proved our techniques were as consistent in Washington as they are in Michigan.

To make sure these results were not just a matter of luck, the next summer I sponsored a fishing delegation of seven other Michigan steelheaders for a trip to these same rivers. This trip found water levels normal, with their rivers holding a tremendous number of steelhead, especially the North Fork of the Toutle. It was also a summer when the temperature hit a torrid 100 degrees for several days and when one thinks about swimming in such blue ribbon steelhead waters, instead of fishing, it's time to head home. We cut the trip short by five days. During this abbreviated trip, we logged 100 1/2 hours, with 76 hook-ups.

During our third summer visit, our hosts guided us to the Garbage Can Hole, on the North Fork of the Toutle. The fishing was so challenging, we logged 56 fishing hours here, putting on a streamside clinic by hooking 68 steelhead. During these 56 hours, we witnessed the locals hooking two fish. But then again, while talking to Jack Ayerst that first trip to Olympia's steelhead headquarters, he stated the average steelheader catches two fish a season. This 1979 trip totaled

158 hours on the river, with 144 hook-ups.

However, while fishing the Barrier Dam on the Cowlitz River, the owner of the local tackle store walked down to inform me he had received a phone call. Tom Janson had been killed in an auto accident. After the initial shock, we folded up the rods and headed the rig toward Seattle, to get me a flight back home. None were available. Nothing was the same after that news.

My final Washington drive came in 1981, the year after Mt. St. Helens blew her top. Of course the Toutle River was destroyed, but we made up for it at our other favorite sites. We ended up fishing 140 hours and enjoyed 142 hook-ups.

I believe anyone would have to agree the results of our first, second, third and fourth visits proved nothing was left to luck. It couldn't get much more consistent than this. It taught us that a steelhead is a steelhead, no matter what geographical area you seek it out. There are no special baits, or special rigging needed to be successful, especially when using long searching leaders in the two and four pound class.

In August, after my last summer trip to Washington, I was invited to fish Indiana's Little Calumet River for Skamanias. Charlie "Steelhead" Myric of Porter, was to fish one day and the next day I fished with the two biologists who were the "baby-sitters" for these monster silver brutes, Bob Koch and Neil Ledet.

The warm temperatures of this slow moving river was stressing some of these aggressive migrators. I found a few dead, then witnessed a few in their final throes. I stood watching Charlie toss his Mepps spinner at one fish who was on its side, struggling to right itself. I couldn't believe he was trying to catch this fish. In fact, the thought crossed my mind, "Is he trying to snag it?" As he guided his spinner toward the fish, I watched the fish, still on its side, move to the spinner and grab it! I could not believe my eyes! Who would believe this?

In addition to this fete, Mike McKee, told me of his new habit when floating nightcrawlers on bobbers in Trail Creek. When he spots a fish, he tosses upstream, then watches the crawler come toward the lunker. If the animal ignores it, Mike will continue the drift, because once in a while he will see the fish turn, sprint downstream to annihilate the crawler. No other strain of steelhead will display such aggression.

A unique Hoosier Skamania happening occurred when Tom Hamilton, of Montigue, Michigan, also Chief Honcho for the Feds lamprey program in the Great Lakes, was fishing the Little "Cal." He must have hooked one of those hellions I had on that 50 to 60 fish day with Bob and Neil. It took off downstream as Tom stood his ground. The panic stricken bullet pulled a 180 on him and as it gained more speed, it exploded from the river, torpedoing him in the chest! Needless to say, Tom quickly became baptized in the name of Skamania Mania!

I listened to the most unique trolling encounter on my radio, where one boater was telling his buddy how one Skamania shot out of the water, killing itself by smashing into the downrigger arm.

The late Jack Parry, Outdoor Editor of the Gary Post Tribune, reported his friend had a torpedo attempt to blow up the turning prop of the motor. Ugh!

Steelhead normally spend a year to a year-and-a-half in the hatchery. When released in a river, they find their way downstream, into the Great Lakes, where they normally spend two to three years. They return to their river as adult spawners at three-and-a-half to four-and-a-half years old.

The length of time steelhead spend in our Great Lakes before they spawn is the most important time of their life cycle. This is when they attain their maximum growth. When they leave the lake and enter the rivers, the rigors of spawning are so demanding on their body, very, very few survive.

Those few that do survive, gain very little in length or weight for the rest of their life.

The time spent feeding in the ocean, or Great Lakes, is such a determining factor in its size, Washington scientists attempted to design another strain of steelhead, a strain that would spend four years in the Pacific before making their first spawning run. They revered to it as a "four- salt" fish. To date, nothing has developed in this attempt.

Meanwhile, Indiana discovered their Skamania developed its own classes of age groups. Koch not only found age groups that spent four years in Lake Michigan before spawning (four-salt), but he discovered Skamanias spending five, or six years in the lake. Bob is the only fish biologist I know who sounded like a big game biologist aging deer, whenever he boasted of steelhead up to six-and-a-half years old!

There was no other steelhead fishery in the world where scores of anglers could catch steelhead averaging 15 pounds every day! There was no other trolling site where a boater could target steelhead for four to six weeks, where scores of trollers had daily catches of steelhead from 18 to 22 pounds.

When Captain Dale Robert (Hammond, IN) and son, Jason, experienced "no show" clients, they fished anyway, landing a record Skamania -26.75 pounds.

Hell, in those days, if a report came over the radio of a catch weighing 18 pounds, I would say to my clients, "So what?" An 18-19 pound fish was "just another steelhead!" If the fish didn't weigh in at 20 pounds, or better, stay off the radio! It was truly a steelheader's paradise!

Notice the above facts about the size of Indiana Skamania is in the past tense? So what happened? It is so basic, the answer is easy.

While it took many years for Washington fish scientists to develop this early-run gene pool, it only took a few years for Indiana to attain the same level of fish science that Michigan had already exemplified.

Michigan blew it when we mixed the Alaskan strain coho with the Oregon strain. The resulting Michigan coho developed into a fall runner and downsized to average five pounds.

Indiana ignored the late May, early June, runs of Skamania at their portable weir site in Trail Creek, even when Koch theorized their big fish showed up earlier! The weir did not go in until significant runs of fish were detected, which was in September and August. It wasn't worth the effort to leave the weir in place, spot check it, then take those May-June fish and hold them in a separate pond. Kiss that "giant size" gene pool goodbye. With that gene pool gone, a record catch is now just another freak fish.

In 1990, I was chartering out of Indiana's Burns Harbor, when my friend, Charter Captain Dale Robert, had a "no show." Since he and his son, Jason, were ready to fish anyway, the two of them set lines the minute they cleared the break wall. Before the morning was over, Jason boated a new Great Lakes Skamania record—26.75 pounds.

However, on July 10, 1993, Kyle Johnson of Wheaton, Illinois was chartering out of Waukegan, Illinois, when he boated a 31 pound 6 ounce mega-monster! Illinois biologist, Rich Hess, aged this Indiana Skamania at eight to 10 years

99

old.

My enthusiasm over this Skamania, caused me to begin writing about these unbelievable experiences. I not only wrote to inform other steelheaders, I also wrote to our Assistant Fish Chief, Dave Borgeson. I had Dave join me in Indiana for a first hand experience with this fish. With some help from others, Michigan finally requested Skamania eggs from Indiana.

My enthusiasm also reached New York's Chief Biologist for Lake Ontario, Les Wedge. A friend and noodle rod charter captain on their Finger Lakes, Bill Haessner, brought Les to Indiana to see this dynamic performer for himself. And see he did—on the end of a 13 foot noodle rod, beefed up to six pound test. They took home their catch of lunker Skamanias for Les to show his biologists. He later called to say it was the best tasting salmonid had has ever had.

Once Michigan was about to make its first plant of Skamanias, I ended up playing a roll in a most interesting event. It took place while I was fishing spring steelhead at Tippy Dam. The siren had sounded, indicating the dam

Warm water temps stress these summer steelhead, so steelheaders know they must keep their fish.

would begin blowing water, so I was on my way to the nearby Wellston Inn where a long-time friend, John Westley, was manager. While chowing down, Bob Kusibab, proprietor of the finest fishing shop in the area, came in to eat. He no sooner sat down when he said:

"Dick, did you hear they are going to release the Skamania in the (Manistee) harbor. Lud Frankenberger, (District Fishery Biologist) will be there with the press to record the event."

I came out of my chair. "They're going to do what... plant those fish in the harbor?" This encouraged Bob to repeat it. I immediately asked John if I could use the phone, then proceeded to call Andy Pelt, Executive Director of the Michigan Steelheaders Association. I burned his ears and he said he would get right on it.

Then I called Dave Borgeson, thinking it would be a cold day in hell to catch him in, let alone have him accept my call. I was most pleasantly surprised when he answered.

My major concern was for the safety of that first plant of Skamania. It is no secret that a large part of all fish planted at harbor sites are devoured by the voracious sea gulls. The conversation went like this:

Me: "How can you plant those fish where the gulls will kill them off?"

Dave: "I don't think it will be that bad."

Me: "Do you have any studies on how long it takes these highly socialized plants to disperse?"

Dave: "Yeah, in about two hours."

Me: "That's too long. Why don't you pick a site upstream?"

Dave: "If you are that concerned, why don't you get a bunch of your buddies, go out on the pier and wave sheets, shoot guns, yell, holler...anything to scare the gulls?"

I could not believe our Assistant Chief of Fisheries was saying this...and he was serious. He was so serious, I beckoned John to share the ear-piece with me. I wanted a witness!

Me: "You have to be kidding! C'mon, plant them up at High Bridge."

Dave: "There are too many predators upstream, we will lose more upstream."

Me: "That's wrong. The only fish in the river that might be on the feed are a couple of Northerns and they may be still spawning."

Dave: "Well, what about the walleyes?"

Me: "They're no problem! They are spawning."

Dave: "I don't know if I can have the truck change its schedule."

At this, I knew he was running out of ammo, trying to tell me some guy who schedules the hatchery tankers, is going to tell the Assistant Fish Chief, "So sorry!"

Dave: "You know if we lose these fish in the river it is going to be your fault!"

I not only felt like the winner, but felt very complimented by having him rest the fate of this plant of my favorite fish on my shoulders. They still dump them at High Bridge. A reported sideline of this event was that Lud and the press were not notified of the change in plant sites and were left waiting at the harbor.

Once Michigan got with the Skamania program, we went one step farther into summer steelhead. We had 300,000 eggs shipped from Oregon. This total represented three different genetic strains of summer steelhead. One was from the Siletz River, from these 100,000 eggs could come steelhead called two salt fish, attaining weights from five to nine pounds.

Another was from their North Umpqua River, these 100,000 eggs were from two to three salt adults, reaching lengths from 26 to 31 inches. The remaining 100,000 were from the famous Rogue River. These eggs would produce the smallest fish of the three. They were from one salt adults called "half pounders."

Along with this shipment of Oregon eggs came 200,000 eggs from Indiana. However, another hatchery problem, this time at our state-of-the-art Wolf Lake Hatchery, reduced the total of 500,000 eggs to 230,000.

Since the Indiana fish had shattered the growth records of Washington's, there was a good chance our Oregon steelhead eggs would follow suit and outgrow their Pacific parents.

We had no intention of collecting eggs from any of these Oregon fish. It was a one shot deal. They were fin clipped and the catch reports showed no real claim to fame on their sizes.

However, the Hoosier progeny sure have gained their claim to fame with Michigan, Illinois, Wisconsin, New York, Pennsylvania and Ontario steelheaders. Like in Indiana, these fish opened a new river season for the rest of us.

Because we have more rivers than other states, Michigan river rats are the most intense. However, although we have this nice distribution of rivers receiving summer-runs, the past six summers have proven to me that the Big Manistee River is the choice site in Michigan. This river selection is not based on the number of planted summer fish the "Big M" receives, but on its past performance, especially at Tippy Dam.

Since Indiana has its new cold water hatchery on the St. Joe River, this river will receive plants of over 225,000 Skamania each spring. That alone should put the St. Joe first on anyone's steelhead list. However, with the recent opening of all five fish ladders, the first ladder, located at Barrien

Springs, Michigan, will remain open for the first three years. This is to get a firm handle on the effectiveness of the different ladders during migration time.

Barrien Springs Dam is the only steelhead site for wading anglers. It offers such a small area for waders, it is a bear to fish. This shortage of wading space finds the river dominated by boats. Regardless, when the ladder is open, these silver locomotives ramrod up and over.

Keep in mind, although these fish are geared to run the rivers in June and July, they don't spawn until winter. Since they are six to seven months away from spawning, when these fresh babies come shooting into a river, their batteries are fully charged and their gas tanks are filled with high-octane. Their tremendous after-burner offers a peduncle which is impossible for even Air Jordan to palm. The only thing that can slow these marathon runners is warm water temperature.

To better illustrate their marathon river runs, Washington fish hit the rivers in late May, early June, reaching their sanctuary waters located at the top of the Cowlitz and Kalama before mid-July. Then again, Washington's cooler summer water temperatures are maintained by glacial melt, these cooler temperatures really rev their engines. In contrast, Michigan's warmer summer temperatures cause fish to pause in the cooler water of tribs. When you hook one of our warm water fish, like in the Indiana, be prepared to keep it.

When I chartered out of Indiana and had a bad day, I headed to Barrien Springs and witnessed the highs and lows of this wading site. This is not to say the river is devoid of fish with the ladder open, but I'll bet a dollar far more fish stage in the unchartered river above Barrien Springs. When this occurs, those upper river fish are "home free."

I had a St. Joe area biologist dispute this "home free" prediction. He sounded like the rest of the Fishery Division when they want to move fish over barriers. Their battle cry becomes, "It will open more water for fishermen to enjoy." Wrong! The classic example of this type of fiasco took place on the Betsie, in 1973, when they dynamited Homestead Dam. Today, the only anglers fishing these new waters are the six area guides and a few waders. The shoulder-to-shoulder crowds continue to fish below the lamprey weir, where the dam used to be.

This St. Joe biologist may know his fish, but he sure doesn't know about crowds. Since I helped invent our crowds, believe me, steelheaders are creatures of habit. We continue to fish the public areas of rivers that continue to produce fish, crowd or no crowd.

There has been only one exception to this movement in crowds of steelheaders. This was when some 800,000 steelhead were planted in our little Rogue River, a tributary of the Grand River and 10 miles northeast of Grand Rapids. It takes an astronomical plant such as this to draw established anglers from their favorite river haunts. I dare our Fishery people to keep a fishing census for the next few years, above Barrien Springs and a census below, then publish it. Of course, with Indiana's stocks of Skamanias in the St. Joe, it is only the fact that the fish ladder will remain open that takes away from making this river number one in the state.

Aside from Tippy Dam becoming a permanent barrier where Skamanias collect, there is room for hundreds of waders. The Big M is as long as the St. Joe, with room for as many boats.

For the past six summers, Skamanias have hit Tippy Dam before the end of June. However, for the past six summers the snaggers have been able to rip salmon from these same waters. Their snagging began September 10 to October 25 and their non-discriminating snagging hooks have ripped almost every summer fish from the site. I religiously begin fishing Tippy on the 26th and have yet to see a Skamania taken by sport fishers. Now for the brighter side of this deplorable situation at Tippy—snagging in all Michigan rivers was banned last year. However, since we experienced a very poor return of Skamania through the summer, our September-February steelhead success at Tippy was nonexistent. But, let me tell you about a rejuvenated sport fishing site for chinook! Wow! It was like the late 60s, before snagging, with shoulder-to-shoulder crowds leading fish down, rather, fish leading them down the river, one after the other.

However, with a recent increase of skamania plants in the Big Manistee, summer and winter steelheading can only get better.

Returning fish from the plant of 800,000 steelhead in the Rogue River guaranteed limit catches of five steelhead to anyone who could land their bait in the river.

Thermal Bar Steelhead
Chapter 10

"Fish starboard at 2 o'clock," came the yell. "I see 'em," acknowledged Duke Edwards, of Wheeling, Illinois, as his spoon was looping through the air in a cut-'em-off-at-the-pass direction. It took three cranks on the 6:1 spinning reel to gather the arching slack out of the line. Four turns later, the rod jolted as a mass of silver fury launched skyward. It was a spectacular sight! Its skyrocketing body soared to at least eight feet, then gracefully nosed over into a power dive which would have scored a 10 from even a Russian judge. In a blink, the silver bullet took another shot at the sun, but coming up short, fell to the surface in a very ungraceful belly-flop.

Duke became a gibbering idiot as he attempted to give a blow-by-blow commentary of the unfolding drama. It wasn't until its seventh leap that a head-shake loosed the spoon. "Unbelievable...unbelievable," came Duke's wrap up.

This steelhead scenario is just one of 10, 20, 30, yes, even over 40 episodes which can take place aboard one boat, in one day, when trolling on our thermal-barriers, on Lake Michigan. Once one of these thermal-barriers (thermo-bars, T-bars, etc.) is located, such steelhead action is the norm, if the fish are there. It is really difficult to believe the number of multiple hook-ups on just one pass through one of these bars. When you know there are many of these thermo bars,

holding thousands of steel-head, you can better understand the dynamics of such a trolling fishery.

Thermal barriers are not to be confused with thermoclines, even though both terms relate to temperature and temperature breaks. Both differ in that thermal barriers relate to surface temperatures and thermoclines, depth. When looking for T-bars, you watch the (surface)

temperature gauge and when watching the thermocline, you look at a graph. Of course, in today's electronic boom, one instrument can give you both.

Locating thermal bars requires an eye peeled on the temperature gauge as you run farther from shore. If you are running out in warm water, you are looking for a sudden cooling of two or more degrees. If you are running out in cold water, then look for a sudden warming. The ideal situation is running out in surface water temperatures at 65 degrees and then as you near the 10 mile reading on your Loran or GPS, see the gauge suddenly drop to 55 degrees. This is it. Many times you see an area of slick water ahead. A slick is always a good indicator of a possible temperature break. They come in all sizes and shapes, but even if the slick shows a dramatic temperature change, it doesn't guarantee steelhead are gathered there. However, work it to death before moving farther out.

I am a stickler for slicks, because I base my fishing on being able to see fish working the surface. Surface action is common at this time of summer, due to insects hatching and dying. Like any inland lake full of rainbow trout, insects

become the only diet for these mean-machine, big water rainbows. Like any inland lake rainbow trout, these silver torpedoes cruise along the surface, in 600 feet of water, with their dorsal fins cutting "V's" as they slurp flies. When I do find a good temp break on a slick, there are times when there is no surface action. This is when, as a last resort, I put two flat lines out 80 feet, with No. 5 J Plugs.

I troll "J's" at 3 1/2 m.p.h., to cover water faster. Any steelhead hitting a J-Plug trolled at this speed, is swimming in the upper 20 feet, because the "J" is digging at least 10 feet. Since J-Plugs are made to slide up the line, away from the mouth of the fish, the leverage for rejection is gone. This depth makes a 3/8 to 1/2 ounce casting spoon eligible to get slammed, but because of its weight-at-the-mouth, it can be wham, bam, thank you...goodbye!

When a steelhead is hooked on a "J," once again, the Lite Liner stops and the other rod is quickly hauled in. While one client fights the fish, the others begin casting spoons, away from the fighting fish. If a problem arises with multiple fish on, it can be easily solved because the boat is dead in the water.

In 1990, I regretfully had to give up on the Skamania trolling fishery in Indiana. The fish had changed their inshore habits and my last two summers were zero. I felt I had to give it at least two summers before being convinced it was a real change and not just a one summer fluke. This is when I decided to stay involved with my favorite fish in

Michigan, even though it meant a 20 mile run into 600 feet of water, instead of dropping lines the minute you cleared the pier heads, in 10 feet of water. I decided to run out of the port of Onekama for my baptismal in this long-distant fishery. Onekama was home base for three captains, whom I call "The Big Three."

They had been the most heralded captains for getting results on the bars. I figured I would be closer to their radio range and could pick up pointers as they communicated—and believe me, Michigan charter captains do keep the airways hot with helpful information. They talk turkey, there are no secrets.

I did not plan to charter this first summer. I just wanted to see how effective my new methods would be in this new water environment. This would mean having my wife, some outdoor writers and many die-hard steelheaders on board the Lite Liner during these maiden voyages. These included my long-time friend, Duke, also a retired educator, helping out during this summer stay. My wife and Duke were along for the first trip out to "Never-Never Land." After about one hour of running at 3,000 r.p.m., we began scouting for sizable slicks. Leaving our 68 degree water and watching the temperature gauge drop to 56, Duke took the wheel, while Chuck and I dropped in the J-Plugs. It took three minutes before the 13 footer on her side tried to leave the boat. The missile was airborne more than it should have been, so I called, "Skamania," as I whipped in the other rod and started to put it in the reserve rod holder. As I reached over, I spotted a "Vee" 20 feet out. I couldn't believe I hit the rod holder hole with the rod, because it seemed I had the spinning rod in my hand, with the spoon on its way before I let it go. It was a perfect cast too. I didn't have time to congratulate myself before the rod wanted to leave my hand. By now, Duke had rolled out of the seat and was coming at me, armed with the other spinning rod.

During this very fast sequence of fish related events, my wife kept yelling at us..."Look at the size of my fish... Hey, you guys, did you see that jump?...did you see how big it is?...Wow, look at the size of this fish"...and on and on and on!

As Duke closed the gap, I instinctively jammed my bent spinning rod into his hand, grabbing the rod out of his other hand. He snugged up to the side of the boat attempting to get control of the crazy gyrating animal, with me right on his butt. One quick look told me where his fish was doing its thing and before my eyes could turn away, my spoon was automatically on its way.   Meanwhile, Chuck had not stopped complaining about our total disregard in looking at the size of her fish. I remember her final words. "Look, you guys, it's right here by the boat. Awww, it's off."   I   don't think I made two cranks on the reel when, whammo and off it went into the wild blue, while Duke was already into the "slug it out" phase of the battle. As Chuck was putting her rod away, still complaining, my fish was out of the water, jackknifing like a tarpon, when the spoon went flying higher than the fish. Talk about a Chinese fire drill! I swear this started and finished in less than 90 seconds. We ended up landing six more steelhead on the plugs, releasing four (not "long line" releases either) on spoons.

Back at the dock, the owner was pumping gas for me and asked how we did. I gave him our creel report. He then made a comment that prompted my usual reply.

"Well, when we can boat seven steelhead, fishing just two lures, I expect those who troll with four lures to take 14 and charter captains running their legal 12 lures, to take 42!" His thoughtful reply was, "I guess I never thought of it that way."

Whenever we see "Jaws" cruising the surface with fly fishers on board, we naturally turn to casting flies, instead of spoons. However, the ideal situation, but seldom occurring,

is finding a scum line loaded with dead insects. This is the time when the fly boys can be assured of casting to steelhead holding in one area, instead of cruising fish.

A scum line is just that, a line of trash floating out in no man's land. This phenomenon occurs where conflicting surface currents (conflicting temperatures) of various magnitudes collect and pile debris, moving it along the surface like a broom. These conflicting temperatures can vary a dramatic 15 degrees. Among the debris, you can see wood, tree trunks, roots, boxes, mattresses, dead animals and birds. It is not unusual to open up the stomach of these lunkers and mixed in with a huge bolus of insects, you might find a bird. However, be very careful when moving a boat through this junk, you may not see something under the surface that can shut you down, 20 miles off shore. This long distant, thermal-bar, steelhead fishery developed as a result of the demise of our Lake Michigan chinook salmon. While this drop in chinook stocks drove many charter captains out of business, others struck out to see if we had this type of fishery in Lake Michigan, like New York trollers found in Lake Ontario.

We are going into our seventh year of guaranteed limit catches of thermal bar steelhead. While this deep water fishery basically involves fleets of boats out of Manistee, Onekama and Frankfort, there are days when we hook-up with Wisconsin fleets out of Sturgeon Bay and Algoma. Do you care to estimate the catch on a day when our two fleets meet, when our limit catch is three per person (including captain and first mate) and with Wisconsin still keeping five fish each? The score can be staggering—for one day of trolling!

Our Fisheries pathologist, John Nath, is diligently working with the chinook's BKD ailment and is finally armed with a cure, Erythromycin, but there are still mixed feelings about whether they can be brought back to the "good ol' days" status. There is also mixed feelings regarding which direction the trolling fleet would go if chinook did make a comeback. It amounts to:

Do you troll inshore, saving gas, while you battle the heaviest bulldogging-freight train in Lake Michigan?

Do you troll 20 miles offshore, burn the same gas you are now accustomed to, while you get burned by the most dynamic aerial acrobat, sprint champion in Lake Michigan?

What would be your choice? Me too!

With the help of fellow outdoor writers, my fishing articles and the sport shows, I maintain a pretty high profile in our Great Lakes fishery.

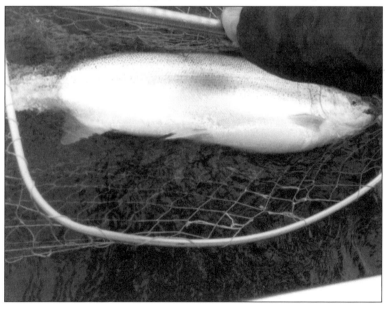

Fly Fishing—A Better Way
Chapter 11

I t was late September when I timed my arrival at the river so I wouldn't need a flashlight to guide me through the state forest. It was a chancy trip because I wasn't sure if the chinook had reached these upper reaches of the Pere Marquette River. It was also chancy to arrive so late because my "honey hole" could already be occupied. But, it wasn't imperative that I fish on this trip, it was just a scouting venture to see if the fish were in. Living close to a blue ribbon river makes scouting more feasible at this early time of the season.

As I approached the upper portion of the pool, I saw two anglers standing some 40 yards downstream. While they fished, the crisp autumn air served as a direct connection to their conversation. Their "no action" report came through loud and clear.

After completing a tie on my terminal rig, I stripped line off the reel then delivered the yarn fly upstream from my pet overhang. The line soon hesitated and I responded with the rod. The river parted with a rip-roaring behemoth. The eruption quickly got the attention of my neighbors, so there was no need to announce the sudden event. After gathering in

their tackle, they stood to watch the show. Another searing run signaled the runaway train was about to invade their section of the river.

As the speed merchant neared

the first angler, I pointed the rod at the fish, grabbed the fly line and broke the fish off. There was no doubt in my mind, the fish was foul hooked and I didn't need to land a fish anyway. I tied another leader, a yarn fly and a second delivery resulted in a repeat performance, along with the long line release. By now my two neighbors were really buzzing and then, I kid you not, a third cast was a replay. This brought a determined comment from one of them, "I'm going over and talk to that guy!"

While I was tying another rig, the visitor approached, pulled up some river bank estate, seated himself and began, "Do you mind...?" He introduced himself as the owner of a sport shop and a TU officer from Dayton, Ohio.

At the end of my streamside clinic, I bit off my rig, then handed him my 8 foot, Berkley XT four pound leader, the No. 12 yarn fly and a Slinky. I also offered him the honey hole, since I saw all I needed. I then wished him well and headed for home.

During the 60 mile hike to Clare, I registered a series of flashbacks back to the 60s, when I was at Midland Bullock Creek. Those were the years when the Pere Marquette received its renewed runs of steelhead and I was spending many hours at Scientific Anglers, talking about it with the late Rod Towsley. I recalled him telling me about some of the noted fly fishers he would entertain on the P.M. and how some of them would pinch split shot on their leaders. The manner in which he talked about it, I knew it was a no-no in the traditional world of fly fishing.

We know this tradition stems from the West Coast, where their philosophy is, "Big fish require big tackle." This translates into casting large diameter fly line to penetrate the river current. This is a far cry from dropping a floating line and dry fly on a river, but even then you must mend the large diameter line. Since spring steelhead and fall salmon don't rise off the bottom to take flies, they must be presented at fish eye-level.

Deep water express, fast sinking, medium sinking, slow sinking and sinking tip lines are a choice for helping to get the fly down to these bottom hugging lunkers. Sections of lead-core line, piano wire, etc., tied in-line in a tapered leader also helps get a fly down into the strike zone. Of course, weighted flies are another way to go. These alternatives can be fished singly, or in combination. However, those who cast these weighted terminal rigs can also experience discomfort when false casting. This discomfort can show as wear-and-tear on the arm and more importantly, it increases the opportunity for you being gored by a low flying hook. If you think of where we are today, these daring celebrities, who fished with Rod, have become the fore- runners of what has come and what I am about to lay on you.

I obviously believe it is only fitting that new techniques arise from new, unique fisheries. One big reason for our making adjustments in tackle is because of our different types of water, compared to West Coast waters. Our headwaters, flow rates, seasonal water temperatures, etc., create innovative approaches. Our geographical make-up is more diversified: therefore, offering the most contrasting salmonid fishing sites, sites I have already covered. As you have noted in each chapter, all of these sites require a number of different techniques in order to enjoy hook-ups.

My break from tradition began in 1980, when I decided it was about time to push what I learned spin fishing, for fly fishers to enjoy, just as spin fishers now enjoy fishing with longer, fly action rods.

The following rationale for prescribed adjustments is applicable to most streams: however, the suggested fly rigs may not be legal in your state waters:

Lead Weights: Since those early days when Rod was telling me about some of his guests using split shot, it slowly appeared to be coming into its own. When Jim Teeney had

his article on split shot come out in *Outdoor Life*, I thought, "Here we go."

Those who have already added shot on their leaders may find themselves spending more time out of the water adding more shot after losing it on bottom estate. This has been one of the necessary evils when doing what is necessary to keep the fly drifting at fish eye-level. However, for the past six seasons, I have been fishing a West Coast weight which has certainly revolutionized bottom bouncing. It is the Slinky Drifter.

It was seven years ago, when we met my friend, Kim Kupniewski, golf pro from Erie, Pennsylvania, in Syracuse, New York. I had another long-time fishing friend with me, Jim Stepulkoski, of Flint. I was doing a sport show in Syracuse and the two were to help me talk about noodle rods and man the booth during my seminar. I always mix business with pleasure at most of my winter shows and when it comes to Syracuse, we always hit the Salmon River in Pulaski.

Kim was telling us all about this new weight he has been

fishing. It sounded like a snow job, but then again Kim was no slouch with a steelhead on. Jim and I told him we would have to see this Slinky Drifter in action, in the morning, on the Salmon.

At the end of the day, Jim went through split shot on almost every cast, while Kim came off the river with the same Slinky he started with. It was still too good to be true.

The Slinky is a combination of hollow parachute cord stuffed with lead shot and comes in a kit. You make them up at the different lengths you think your rivers require, after cutting these to the desired length, burn the nylon ends and seal them with a pair of pliers.

It requires a snap swivel to pin behind the weld, then I run my butt leader through the eye, making it a slip sinker. Tie a barrel swivel on the butt leader. This becomes the stopper for the sinker and the other eye of the barrel is for the tippet.

Fly Line: To help eliminate the added friction caused when large diameter fly line penetrates the current, I opted to come as close to my eight pound test monofilament main line as possible. So, when I saw Leon Chandler, retired president of Cortland fishing lines, at one of the Syracuse sport shows, I ran all of this by him. He sent me a spool of his .031 diameter No. 1 running line. Later, I talked to Bruce Richards, 3M's technical advisor at Scientific Anglers. He sent me a spool of his .029 diameter No. 1 running line. I was now armed with the thinnest diameter fly line on the market.

Bruce also mentioned to me that he was working with Ray Schmidt, a noted river guide, on another type of line, just for this method of fly fishing. When he handed me his .025 diameter intermediate shooting line, he added, "Dick, you know we are getting closer to spin fishing." However, he had a nagging problem with the coating stripping off and later removed it from the market place. But, we still fish with the thinnest fly line to overcome friction and the pressure created from it.

My most vivid, never-to-be-forgotten example of what pressure alone can do, takes me back to the early 70s when our Michigan Fisheries Division sent a tanker to Quebec, to bring home 20,000 Atlantic salmon smolts. My respect for this leaper began in 1966, when our summer vacation in New Brunswick, gave me two weeks of fishing such rivers as the Restigouche, Nippissiquet, Renous and the Big South of the Miramichi. Chuck would drop me off for each day of fishing, then entertain our four budding little ones.

Our Fisheries people then planted 10,000 in the AuSable River and 10,000 in the Boyne River—Everett Kirchner's river. It was his love for this fish which initiated this whole effort. He purchased the initial 10,000 fish and the Fisheries Division got the rest for us. But it was Everett's Boyne River which I zeroed in on.

During the first open season, it was flies only on the Boyne, with all fish taken in the river (an imaginary line across the mouth) to be released. I had spotted fish moving in and out of the Lake Charlevoix mouth on Memorial Day week- end and called Janson. Tom, Marty and I were there bright and early the next Saturday.

I had my Atlantic flies, all tied on double hooks, in sizes 10 and 12. Tom and Marty opted to fish the lake side of the mouth with spinners and spawn bags with bobbers, where they were allowed one fish per day.

I was standing on a 12 inch I-beam in downtown Boyne City, below a five foot culvert, making short casts across this 15 foot wide piece of river. When a small pod of fish came in they were very easy to see and it was very frustrating to see these streamline silver demons loom before your very eyes. They were easily identified as they swam by, because they all shared a common flaking of scales near their dorsal fin.

Each time Tom or Marty would tell me when fish were coming and I would have my No. 12 Rusty Rat in the air,

Assembled Slinky Drifter Rig

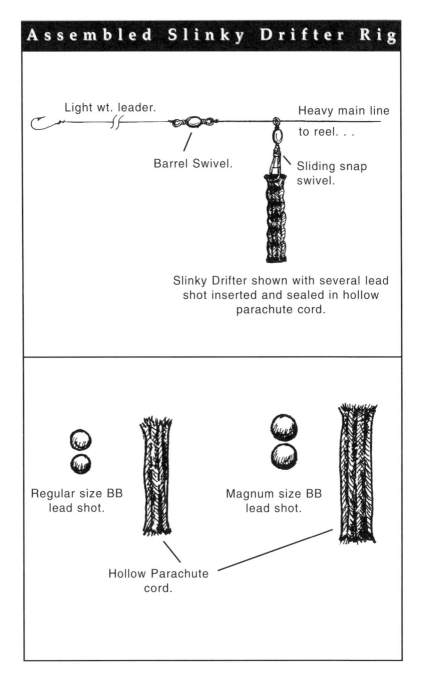

Light wt. leader.

Heavy main line to reel. . .

Barrel Swivel.

Sliding snap swivel.

Slinky Drifter shown with several lead shot inserted and sealed in hollow parachute cord.

Regular size BB lead shot.

Magnum size BB lead shot.

Hollow Parachute cord.

eager to make a presentation. In anticipation of greeting this one, I would actually have the fly on the drift as it approached. When I noticed a hesitation in the drift, I flicked the rod tip and a rocket-propelled Salmo salar jettisoned a good three feet above my head. Now, I stand 6'4" and was standing on this 12 inch beam. It was an unbelievable sky reaching effort. Upon entry, I was showered with the geyser of water. It was a free fish before it left the water. With the diameter of the fly line and speed of the fish against the current, I didn't have a chance. I experienced the same dilemma fishing a sinking shooting head in New Brunswick. Beef up the leader? I hope by now you understand the necessity of hooking a fish first, before worrying about landing it.

One of my most memorable experiences with this Boyne River silver dynamo and two pound test searching leaders occurred in July of '75, when Chuck and I took a Sunday drive to Boyne City for a look at the river. I was thinking big and had her bring a camera along. It would be great to get pics with her into one of these bullets.

It was a clear, sunny day and when we arrived at the bridge, it was downright hot. In fact it was so hot, I slipped on a pair of rubber flippy-flops and a pair of lighter pants. Like any steelheader looking for fish in such shallow critical water, we headed for the dam. The white water would offer the fish cover from the blazing sun, as well as a better supply of oxygen. We didn't eyeball anything, so I began fishing my pet drift.

The rules had changed since my first trip with Tom and Marty. The fish biologists were having problems with this delicate species , so instead of just having them die from an unidentifiable stress, we were allowed to keep them.

It wasn't long before I had a cork-screwing animal heading downstream. I put the legs in gear and didn't get far before the fish broke off on something. I went down to look, since I had never had that problem before. While looking things over, I spotted a fish holding on the far side. I asked Chuck if she wanted a go at it, but she said she would rather get it on camera. I thought that was pretty positive thinking and began working on the silver ghost.

I felt comfortable with the fish, and more importantly, it was comfortable with me...or the searching leader. If there was a time when a fish should have been on red-alert, this was it, but it continued to tolerate my presentations.

When the fish "took," it did not mess around! It created a scene resembling an animal not knowing which direction to go to get out of the river. I stood paralyzed until it got straightened out and tore downstream. I was sure it was too fast for her to get pictures, but I was more interested in where my feet were stepping.

The fish was so far away, I sensed trouble and when I rounded a bend, I saw the trouble. It was a windfall and the line felt anchored to it. I got into the tree, pulled the line taut and ran the rod tip down to the fly. This was a risky move with the rod. If the guide caught on something, that would be bad news. I broke the line and went to shore to talk it over with my camera lady. I was a nervous wreck.

She told me she got some shots of the chase and I suggested we go eat a late lunch. We took our time, because I wanted to look over the water, just in case. When we reached the bridge, we stopped for a good look and there it was. It had to be the same fish because I never saw any Atlantic swim through the culverts. Every one I witnessed at the mouth of the river would swim across the opening, turn back downstream and into the lake. Those fish just swam in a circle. Yes, they had to swim through to reach the dam, but I never saw it happen. With this in mind, I was thinking big, because this was a big fish. It had to be the same fish. It stopped because of the culvert. But would it panic again and shoot through this time?

With a new shot of adrenaline, I rigged-up and worked

myself into position. After all, hooking the same steelhead we release is old hat. As long as any migrator holds in the current, it is still eligible. This is the nature of a turned-off, spawn-run fish.

Once again, the fish held solid, as I presented the fly on a fresh searching leader. The second I hooked it, I knew it was the same fish I lost. It was a scrapper, but it just didn't have the flash, or dash. We slugged it out in a 20 foot area, without it even thinking about heading through the culvert. I heard the camera's auto-wind as I reached for its peduncle, but the fighter just had to bow out with class. With my arm extended, it elevated in my face and showered me from its dead fall into the river. This was caught on film. The 14 pound two ounce Atlantic is still listed as the world record Atlantic salmon, in the four pound line class, with Fresh Water Hall of Fame. The two pound XT leader was still too strong after the fight. It tested closer to four pound test.

The suppleness of the No. 1 running line became a problem at the stripper guide. Too often it would grab onto the guide, stopping the delivery in mid-air. There wasn't much I could do about it, after all, it wasn't designed as a casting line.

While attending the '91 Federation of Fly Fishers Conclave, in West Yellowstone, Leon Chandler told me of his new "harder" No. 1 running line, with the same .031 diameter. I knew about the harder Bone Fish Line, which S.A. sells and how that stuff zooms through the guides, so I was fired up at Leon's news. It was also timely news for me to pass on to those attending my seminars that afternoon.

Later in the summer, Bruce informed me of his new "harder" number one line with the .029 diameter. Believe me, it is the answer to the snarled stripper guide syndrome. Those nagging problems are in the past and now I am talking about roll casting up to 60 feet.

Butt Leaders: Because butt leaders are always in the current, their diameters demand the same concern as fly line. When shopping for thinner monofilament leaders, you may consider a Tackle Test magazine report, giving the nod to Silver Thread AN40. It also rates it the best for strength and abrasion. Let me tell you about its abrasion quality.

When I read this report, I picked up some eight pound test for the main line on my spinning reels to help reduce current friction. I took one of the reels to Florida for a 10 day skirmish with tarpon and bone fish. I was a guest of the Jim Bicknell's of Clare, with young Dr. Jim Bicknell and me flying down together. His retired parents have a knock-out residence in Duck Key. Jim's dad, "Big" Jim and his wife, Doris, are both licensed charter captains, out of our port of Ludington.

After nine consecutive days of wind, young Jim and I tossed a spinning rod in the boat and headed out to take a look-see at some flats. We rounded a small island and couldn't believe the number of guides staked out. Since they favored the outside area, Jim headed inshore, poling us in about a foot of water. We had fresh shrimp, with one already impaled on a No. 8 Eagle Claw, style 42 wide bend hook.

We spotted a fish, but my cast didn't get the job done. A third sighting was the charm with the fish taking the shrimp. As it sprinted along the shore, I held the reel up for Jim to see the spool emptying. He got on the pole as the fish slowed to a crawl, then in a second I was hung-up. I couldn't believe this could happen with my first bone. Jim soon arrived at the first problem, where I worked the tip of the rod around this plant, the shape and appearance of a large mushroom. The line came loose and I came back on the rod. No soap, it was hung again. We arrived at the site to see another mushroom was the culprit. Off came the line, but this problem was to stick around for another three mushrooms. Then, there was still another hang-up. This time when we closed the gap, the line was around a spindly piece of coral. It wouldn't come off, so Jim went overboard. Now, you have to picture these staked-out guides and their clients, sitting there doing absolutely nothing, but watching us! So, here was Jim standing in waist deep water. He took a breath and submerged. He came up with the little plant and freed the line. Once back into the boat, we found ourselves on our way to a seventh snag. Once again, with all eyes upon us, Jim had to take another jump into the ocean. It was another one of these little coral spindles. As luck would finally have it, when I came back on the rod, the fish was still there. Once again into the sassy fighter, I mentioned my concern for the poor line, after all of that brutal abuse.

Jim later grabbed the beautiful eight pounder and without out a camera to prove it, he released the fish. The hang-ups sure killed the initial excitement of this first experience, so I took a lighter-side attitude by reminding Jim that he set one hell-of-a precedent for those guides, if their clients ever get hung-up! While the Silver Thread was brutalized, it ended up getting the job done.

To take advantage of such strong, thin butt leader monofilament, I ran it 1 1/2 times the length of the rod. In other words, whenever I fish my 12 foot rod, the butt leader is 18 feet long. Then, of course, I go with a six to ten foot, two to four pound test tippet, coming off the barrel swivel. With 24 to 28 feet of mono in the water and the rod held high, only the monofilament penetrates the current. Even the thin number one running line doesn't get into the drift. Only thin mono is in the drift for spin fishers and now only thin mono is in the drift for fly fishers.

With this long butt leader, strip the fly line until the knot comes through the top guides to the ferrule of the rod. This means with each roll cast the knot shoots through the top guides. To facilitate a smoother, longer cast, I tie an Albright knot instead of the nail knot. The U-shaped fly line at the knot, sneaks through the guides easier than the banging of the stub sticking out of a nail knot. If you paint the knot, it also flies through the guides.

Decide what pound test tippet you will fish, then tie a butt leader which is four pound test heavier. This minimum difference of four pound test will assure you the butt leader will not break off when hung-up. Only the lighter weight tippet will break. If you tie heavier butt leaders, you increase the resistance in the drift. If you tie a lighter weight butt leader, you will have more break-offs at the Albright knot. If you tie a heavy butted tapered leader, you just increased the resistance again. Use level 10 pound test butt leaders when choosing to fish four to six pound test tippets and 10 pound test main line for spin fishers who fish four to six pound leaders. It's the best of both worlds for beating bowed, slack line in a drift.

Rod Action: Once again, the Cardinal Sin of the fly fishing world is the complete lack of concern for stressing balancing a fly rod with the weakest link of the fly tackle—leaders and tippets! With all of the "holier-than- thou" preachings for sport fishing ethics, it is the one fishing community that abuses it unmercifully.

Allow me to take a sur-

Dr. Jim Bicknell chooses a 10 foot IMX, No. 10 fly rod for his in-line leader section of 16FA 12pound test for tarpon.

gical approach to the use of leaders: You are interested in setting an I.G.F.A. record in the eight pound test line class for tarpon. You understand the rules allow you a 15 inch section of the eight pound mono tied into the tapered leader. You also know a shock leader of 100 pound test is recommended to withstand the punishment from the gill plates of a leaping fish. So what rod action do you select? Right, since it is a tarpon you are fishing, you opt for the traditional No. 12 to 13 tarpon fly rod!

Surgically, you will fish a No. 12-13 rod with I.G.F.A. eight pound mono. This eight pound mono is your weakest link. You are grossly out-of-balance.

How about the promoted sporting ethic of not taking too long to land a fish? This out-of-balance fly tackle sure doesn't help the cause.

In all of your reading, have you ever noted where a tarpon fly fisher used a No. 7-8 fly rod with I.G.F.A. eight pound test inserted in the leader, or a No. 10 rod with 12 pound?

I marvel at these tarpon personalities who never bend the rod while fighting the fish. They keep the rod tip low and

A 15 foot, No. 10 Spey rod isn't just for fishing Russia's Ponoi River, and it isn't only for leaders up to 15 pound test.

fight the monster off the reel. That is, until the fish is at the boat, then the rod seems to automatically double over into a "C," because of the lifting effect. At least I can see the action of the rod is parabolic during the landing phase of the game.

Three years ago, I was (again) with Dr. Jim at Duck Key. In preparation for the trip, I tied up a Loomis IMX, 9 foot, No. 13 tarpon blank for bait fishing with mullet. While in a sport shop in Marathon, we overheard a conversation relating to the need for manufacturers to come out with a 20 pound tarpon rod. This was the subject because of I.G.F.A. opening up a 20 pound test class. Jim and I just grinned.

First of all, they never pressure the fish with the full bend of the rod, during the long distant fighting phase anyway. If they did bend a rod, they would know Loomis' IMX No. 13 rod is already a 20 pound tarpon rod.

If they could have watched Jim wrap this No. 13 tarpon rod into a "C" with a seven foot shark and an 85 pound tarpon, on Berkley XT 20 pound test, they would have cringed at the sight of the rod pressure, but they would know Loomis already has a 20 pound tarpon rod. Do you know what? The next year, Gary listed a 20 pound tarpon blank in his catalog! I couldn't believe it!

Allow me to take a surgical approach to the use of tippets: You are fishing the Conservatory waters of Silver Creek in Idaho. You know this shallow pristine water holds big rainbows and an occasional brown trout bordering on eight pounds.

Are you really going to address these fish with 6X-8X tippets on a No. 4-5-6 fly rod?

Do you own a No. 1-2 fly rod to better protect this angel hair tippet...to fish more in-balance?

Trout Unlimited, Federation of Fly Fishers and other fly fishing groups should think about this "baby the fish" syndrome, created by fly fishers who cannot max the rod with their choices of tippets.

Several years ago, a friend sent me a video of one of the "top dogs" in the fly fishing world. He was fishing trout in Wyoming and was narrating as he fished. He mentioned the 8X tippet and the No. 6 rod he was using, as he sloshed around the pool, following the fish, trying to avoid breaking the tippet on a 13 inch fish.

Can you visualize the fly fisher who opts for a fast tip rod, to throw tighter loops with, as he fights a trout on a 4X to 6X tippet? C'mon, give the fish a break. Consider the safe release of the fish, or disturbing other fish in the pool before hooking it, unless you plan to eat it.

It's a good thing fly fishers don't create the large crowds spin fishers do. I can visualize the impatience of a crowd waiting for "Hollywood" to quit show-boating with his slightly bent fly rod! They would renovate his two piece rod into a six piece travel rod!

Opting for number one running line and lead weight eliminates the concern to balance fly line and fly rod. With the lead delivering the fly, the tippet becomes the determiner for balancing fly tackle. None of us ever own enough rods, but every one of those rods normally requires a separate reel, or extra spool, loaded with the balanced fly line. When opting for this alternative method, those several fly rods now require only one fly reel, with no extra spools.

Rod Length-Line Control: Number one running line offers less resistance in a current, but it becomes even lesser when the proper length rod is selected and if it is held high during the drift. The correct rod length, combined with number one running line, can offer a fly fisher ultimate line control.

Holding the rod at 80 to 90 degrees in the air pulls the number one line out of the current, with only the smaller diameter butt leader in the current. When one of these lunker spawners mouth a fly, you will be there—"Fish on!"

But, what length rod should you fish? It has to be a personal choice, because it must feel comfortable to you. But, it should also fit the size streams you favor. In other words, what length rod feels comfortable when you wade small streams, large rivers, or fish from a boat? While it is a personal choice, let me offer some suggestions.

I recommend the rod be a minimum of nine feet for any of the above. Small streams which receive runs of spawning steelhead, or salmon, are big enough and open enough where a nine footer rarely feels unwieldy. I can't think of one such river where you get swarmed on by bushes, overhanging vegetation, etc.

While our P.M., Platte, Betsie, Paw Paw, Rogue, Pentwater, and Bear (Petoskey) Rivers make you feel comfortable with nine foot rods, rods up to 12 feet should be considered for some areas of these waters.

I should qualify the need for a nine to twelve foot rod on these mentioned rivers, since there is a difference between those who wear waders and those who wade. If you have ever fished the "Holy Water" of our Pere Marquette, you know what I am about to say, because you too watch the "hunters" stalking their quarry in the middle of the long, shallow gravel runs. These great wading hunters could do well with a seven foot rod. However, for those of us who know better than to tread in waters over our ankles, a 10-12 foot rod is the greatest.

Big rivers like our Big Manistee, Muskegon, Grand, AuSable and St. Joe, require wading steelheaders to move up to 11-13 foot rods, for natural reasons. It is amazing how an experienced angler, who is not accustomed to gracing such big waters, will feel undergunned the minute he has completed his first cast and drift with a 10 foot rod. It is a helpless feeling when you have no control over the drift, as you watch the long rodders enjoy the fishing action and with a lot less effort.

In June of '93, Marty, Dave Arff and I headed for Russia's Ponoi River. We fished the Upper Camp along with eight Finns and three Germans. They, plus the three Russian guides all wanted to know why Americans fish one-handed fly rods. Think about it! Certainly, we have rivers the size of the Ponoi and other European rivers, where long, two-handed rods are the norm. How many of us, who have fished these rivers, have done what the Romans do and fished these rods?

We didn't! Our new generation IMX 13 foot, No. 8 rod, with a nine inch butt, offered us the same lift and lay casting, with far less fatigue.

High Modulus Rods: Any fly fisher who hasn't considered the graphite "superlites" must be from the younger generation. As the spokesperson for ye ol' river veterans, they sure help ease arthritic joints.

Regardless of age, these rods deserve serious consideration, because of their wide choices of line weight and lengths. For instance, there are graphite superlites up to 13 foot, for line weights No. 3-10, weighing less than yesterday's seven footers. Breaking from matched fly tackle, these translate into handling 6X-15 pound test tippets!

I fish a 12 foot IMX graphite, designed for No. 6 fly line and 4X-2X tippets. It weighs 3.65 ounces. I fish this rod for chinook, standing ankle-deep in the P.M., with number one line, 18 foot, eight pound test butt leader, Slinky and a six foot, 4X tippet. The balanced combination makes for effortless roll casts and with the rod held upwards, the ultimate in line control.

On the Big M, I fish the 13-14 foot IMX graphite rod, with the eight pound test, 21 foot butt leader, 6X tippets, 8-10 feet long. It weighs 4.25 ounces.

Simply put, the higher modulus graphites weigh less because of the density of the material. Loomis compresses his IMX graphite at 47 million P.P.S.I. Gary, who has spearheaded the new generations of these graphites, says his IM6 graphite is 17 percent lighter than regular graphite and his IMX is 37 percent lighter than regular graphite. His latest are two finished rods, rate higher than IMX. It just gets easier for us ol' folks!

Rod Butts: Fighting Butts- I may be wrong, but I thought a butt extension on fly rods was to aid the angler by giving him an added lever to fight a lunker. If this isn't so, then the butt must have been added just for cosmetic effect. "They shore do look purdy with thot thar lil' ol' knob on tha end!"

Because of the leverage required to fight a trophy fish, I came out with a longer rod. If a longer lever gives us the ability to add greater pressure, why not add a longer fighting butt extension to a shorter rod, to handle big fish? So they did. Or did they? Let's look at the infamous tarpon rod again.

Have you ever seen a fighting butt on a tarpon rod longer than four inches? Aren't they really more often two inches than four? But then again, just what added leverage does either give you?

Whenever a fly client asks me for a long detachable fighting butt, I extend the reel seat two inches off the end of the blank. This suffices for accepting any length fighting butt. In the early days of graphite reel seats, since these were the lightest weight reel seats, I installed them on all of my rods,

With no fighting butt on his 10 foot, No. 4 rod, it is easy to see the discomfort this Pere Marquette River chinook is causing Dr. Bicknell.

including fly rods.

One evening, I received a call from a Toledo rod client telling me he broke the reel seat. I gave him the third degree from every angle I could think of and it still amounted to the fact he broke the seat! Since I have always backed my rod work, I had him ship me the rod. Upon receiving it, I could see he did break the seat. I just chalked it up to one eight inch fighting butt out of how many others? No problem. However, later one fall, my brother Jim, came up from Noblesville, Indiana, to fish chinook on the P.M. River. I gave him my 12 footer, designed for 4X tippets, with a nine inch detachable butt. I was standing alongside when he hit a king and it began burning him bad. When the fish finally took a breather, he pulled the rod into a C. Everything was going along fine, when I heard a "plop" in the water. When I looked, Jim had the rod still bending in one hand, and the nine inch butt in the other. There was no reel! It was the reel I heard go into the drink. What a sight. He was still in awe, because he had not yet figured out what had suddenly made things feel awkward. I honestly thought a foot on the reel broke, pulling it out of the hoods of the seat and into the water.

We were standing ankle deep, so retrieving the reel was no problem, but while all of this thought process was going on, I took the butt and the reel. Jim was doing all right for awhile, but when the fish took off again, I could not line up the reel correctly with the bending rod and the four pound tippet finally parted.

Once again, it was the pressure the nine inch butt exerted that caused the graphite seat to break and not the tippet! Believe it! As a result, I don't install graphite reel seats on rods requiring seven to 10 inch fighting butts. It is impossible to break the same graphite reel seat with a four inch butt, because it is impossible to apply enough pressure.

Since there is no way butts up to four inches play a role in conquering fish faster, companies must install them as a cosmetic thing. But tell me, how cosmetic is it when you see videos with tarpon anglers burying this short butt into their folds of adipose, causing their fingers to massage their flab with each turn of the reel?

In 1970, I came upon some 10 foot blanks from Australia,

which were designed to "C" with 10 pound test. They were great pier rods for casting spoons for chinook.

I got the idea of putting on an extra handle (I called it a "fighting handle"), ahead of the foregrip. However, in a short time, I stopped. I began to think if I wanted an angler to grab onto the fighting handle, I should list the rod as a seven foot rod, instead of a 10 footer. When this higher fighting handle becomes the fulcrum, you destroy the benefit of having the longer rod and its specific action.

You don't need one of these high fighting handles to kill the action. All you need to do is reach up and hook a finger around the blank. I see this happen on rivers more than I care to. It is a bad habit.

The answer to this habit, plus the high fighting handle, is to get a longer butt extension. With one hand on the butt cap and the other near the top corks of the foregrip, your hands are now as wide and as comfortable as they were with the bad habit.

Strike Indicators: Nymph fishers, like steelhead drifters, must have the closest thing to absolute line control, in order to connect with the mouth of a fish holding in deeper water. But, whenever a nymph fisher opts for a strike indicator, he puts himself in the same ball park as a steelheader floating a nymph on a bobber. The item used as the indicator becomes the added resistor in a current, yet I have not witnessed one nymph fisher who was concerned with the amount of line bellying ahead of his indicator. Like the spin fisher who floats a bobber, the nympher must lift the belly off the surface first, before he can sink a hook in the jaw of a fish. That creates a critical pause before being able to strike the fish, one that will cost more missed fish than the angler can imagine. Like those early days at Tippy, the nymph fisher will never know if it was a fish, or the bottom.

Comparing the strike indicator to a bobber is becoming a far easier comparison to make, thanks to the latest fly fisher's "bible," Orvis. Or haven't you noticed their selection of strike indicators? Yes, Bruce Richards, you are correct, we are bordering on spin fishing!

In addition to Orvis offering us those selections of indicators (or bobbers), do you notice their new "harder" No. 1 running line at .029 diameter? Thanks again, Bruce!

Atlantic Salmon Vs. Brown Trout

Chapter 12

K en Darwin, Editor of *Michigan Hunting & Fishing*, and I just arrived in my charter fishing port of Ludington. It was August, 1981 and our adult chinook were returning inshore. In preparation for the morning boat trip, we pulled into a convenience store to pick up some goodies. While Ken did the shopping, I was standing near the front counter when I spotted a picture of the new Michigan record "brown" trout on the front page of the local newspaper. I immediately said to myself, "No way!"

This fish was the second brown trout record caught in about a two week period off the Bathhouse, a popular trolling area out of Ludington. I had seen the picture of the first record fish, but I just glanced at it, thinking nothing of it. After all, a 32 pound brown trout is just another monster brown caught on our side of Lake Michigan.

Charter Captain Jack Duffy, is our Lake Michigan brown trout trolling pro! It was his 31 pound brown record this 32 pound catch dethroned. Then, when I heard this latest 32 pound, 10 ounce fish was taken, I still thought so what? That is, until I saw the picture.

I grabbed Ken and got into his ear, "This is an Atlantic...it's not a brown...it's an Atlantic!"

In the morning we were on the phone, instead of fishing. As a result, we found the fish was at a local taxidermist's shop. We called and were invited to come out to have a look. Upon arriving, he told us he also had the other record fish in the freezer. I wanted to see it too.

He carried the fish out on the lawn and began unrolling their frozen bodies. When the first fish was unwrapped, my eyes targeted the large scarlet marking in the anal area. This coloration appeared on the other fish, also in the anal area. This was more proof than the slightly concave cut in its tail that the fish was an Atlantic.

First of all, a big brown trout never has a dent in its tail. It's either a definite square, or slightly convex—never concave! In contrast, Great Lakes Atlantic salmon never show a square tail! These "football" monsters displayed that slight indentation in their caudal fin. The smaller the Atlantic, the deeper the "V."

Whoever saw scarlet coloration on the bottom side of a brown trout, let alone two brown trout in a row?

While spending those summers on the Boyne River, I caught several Atlantics bearing this scarlet marking. At times it appeared on the throat, at times on the thin membrane of the lower jaw, where a finger would easily tear through. These two fish were the first, where I saw this coloration in the anal area. With more confidence in my "call," Ken and I began a telephone marathon.

I called state fish biologist Steve Swan (no relation), who is the man who baby-sat our Boyne River Atlantics, during those introductory years. I asked if he ever saw the fish, he said Lansing hadn't asked him. I smelled more Lansing politics. I asked him if he ever saw any coloration on the bottom of brown trout. His answer was, "No." I called Myrl Keller, another state biologist. He too had never seen such markings on brown trout.

Ken and I began looking for support from the media. He received immediate support from Dave Richey, Outdoor Editor, Detroit News, as Dave began putting pressure on the Fishery Division to hold off awarding the brown trout record award to the lucky angler who caught the recent lunker. Lansing had already given the award for the 32 pounder caught weeks earlier.

In the meantime, a highly respected charter captain, out of Ludington, was asked to view the fish and render an opinion. He proclaimed both were brown trout! Dave brought in Jack Duffy to see the fish. When Jack tailed the two monsters, swinging them in a circle, he said, Atlantics. Have you ever tried to grab a brown trout around its peduncle? Forget it! This served as more impetus for Dave to go to press against Lansing.

Lansing called in a second Michigan fish biologist to look at the fish. He took "the book" to key the physical character- istics of the fish and came up with, brown trout.

All of this plus our phone calling, got us more media sup- port. Gordon Charles, Frank Mainville (Lansing), Glen Sheppard, all outdoor editors of state papers, began going after Lansing to postpone their presenting the award until some independent authority could render a final decision.

Lansing, as usual, took the stand that no fisherman, or any member of the press, is going to tell them! The award was presented.

A growing barrage of media pressure finally caused Lansing to agree to have Dr. Reeve Bailey, former Taxonomist, at Michigan University, look at the fish and make the determining call on their classification.

Dr. Bailey found both fish were Atlantics. He pointed out that Atlantic salmon and brown trout are "kissing cousins," requiring a close look at their internal organs. That makes scientific sense, since Atlantics are trout and not salmon.

I received a copy of a departmental memo going out to all state fish biologists, labeling me as a "tennis shoe" biologist. I loved it! It also stated, before future state brown trout records are announced, the fish will be examined by an inde- pendent taxonomist.

Too bad other Great Lakes states and Ontario didn't take the hint from our dispute, to avoid finding themselves in the same possible position, because it wasn't too many years later before New York announced a new state record brown trout, while the profile picture revealed the fish as another

Atlantic.

Ken called for my opinion of this fish, then began communicating with New York for a possible independent decision. No way? I called Les Wedge to plead for such an independent finding. He said the fish had already been mounted, but also mentioned the offal from the fish was still frozen. I then reminded him of Dr. Bailey's findings—that keying physical features aren't enough—that it requires an examination of the internal organs to make the final call. I assured him I would keep Darwin off his back, with "see, I told you so, etc," if that was his worry. When I hung up, I was sure I had aroused his scientific curiosity to where he would do it. He didn't! It is just another example of our almost nonexistent scientific desire or curiosity in the Great Lakes area.

Later, a troller from Ontario landed a new record brown trout, just across the lake from New York. Again, from the picture, it was an Atlantic. I mentioned it to Darryl Choronzey, Editor of Ontario Fisherman, but by then I knew it was too late.

In these last two cases, the only winner was the angler, whether it was a record brown trout, or a record Atlantic salmon; however, it was another loss, another scientific setback in the Great Lakes area—and in my opinion, another loss for the coveted Atlantic salmon!

Noodle Rod Impact on
Great Lakes Steelheaders

Chapter 13

L ooking back over these 32 years of steelheading, des-
tiny has served my aspirations very well. The
sequence of fishing opportunities opened more doors
to outdoor editors and freelance writers, all of whom are
great people and continue to support my efforts. As stated
earlier, the culmination of these efforts made it possible for
me to hang up 21 years in education, to pursue the noodle
rod business full time and find time to guide and charter.

These 21 years included 11 years as head football coach,
two years in basketball, 15 years as Athletic Director and in
the final six years, I managed to work myself down to
Assistant Principal, then Principal.

To help move the business along, in 1975, I bought a
booth space at Detroit's Outdoorama sport show. Burl had
already retired from his Principalship and assisted by his
wife Ruth, agreed to man the booth during the week. Even
then, Janson, Marty and I would take off after school and
make a mad dash to Detroit to get involved in the show. The
Swan Rod team wore orange jumpsuits for these shows and
on weekends, the "Orange Men" stole the show. A weekend
at Outdoorama would consist of Tom and his wife Donna,
Archie, Buck, Marty, Burl, Ruth, Chuck and me. The "Orange
Men" in the aisle, bending rods to demonstrate their action,
served as the impetus for 623 rod orders that year. Although
those numbers of rod orders have dwindled over the years, I
continue to hit the winter sport show circuit to preach the
noodle rod-lite line techniques and to book fishing trips. Of
course, the first (1977) never-to-be-forgotten steelhead trip,
was our motor home venture to Washington. Aside from the
camaraderie with the King County group, Loomis and our

Ontario's Saugeen River is due east of Michigan's AuSable River, both are tributaries of Lake Huron.

fishing score, the motor home experience itself, convinced me it was the only way to go. I have owned a motor home ever since, with Michigan FISH ON license plates, to serve my river clients with riverside accommodations.

Before taking that first fantastic summer trip to Washington, John Kerr, an outdoor writer from Toronto, came over in the spring to look over our steelhead streams. After touring our U.P. streams in my rig, we agreed to get together in Canada, in the fall. It was November when he called to report a rain had moved fish into the Saugeen River. He wanted me to bring some of my guys over to enjoy their steelhead, which in reality were our Michigan fish who wandered over to the other side of Lake Huron and stayed. I lined up Mike and Burl for the November 6, quick trip.

We connected with John and he led us into the First Rapids, on a frigid, bright Saturday morning. After fighting

The fast growing fraternity of "float" fishermen is a dedicated one.

more ice in the guides than fish, John decided we should move up to the barrier, Denny's Dam.

It was nearing noon, as we sat in the rig, eating and talking. Suddenly, John exploded from his seat, desperately pointing out the back window, sputtering, "There's a lion... tiger.....!" We all turned, but saw nothing. In the meantime, John continued to rant and rave about what he saw crossing the road. After he settled down, it boiled down to him seeing a mountain lion, one which had already been reported in the area. We took a time-out for him to make a formal sighting report to a ministry officer. With this bit of excitement out of the way, we meandered down to the river.

The sun had warmed the water and also the crowd of people who were busy sifting the water. With both sides of the river loaded with fishermen, we decided to split our forces. Mike cleverly worked his way among those fishing at the dam. John and I strolled down near the Abutments, while Burl moved a short distance below us.

I handed John one of the first graphite rods Loomis designed to "C" with four pound test, without shattering.

John applied one of Archie's famous bobbers to his main line and began floating a spawn bag. "Slurp," went the bobber and John did what any noodle rodder finds easy to do.

"Fish on," went the message to those fishing near us and the nine foot graphite went into its natural bend. John was no slouch with a steelhead on the fighting end of a stick. His streamside clinic ended with a release that created a lot of attention. They just don't release fish on the Saugeen.

We then watched Burl milk a real beauty for the crowd. He loves attention and his down-home ways had the crowd loving it. When he finally finished his chores, a slab-sided 12 pound eye-opener graced the bank.

As John and I were talking about his fish, a steelheader walking by, saw my vest and offered, "Your buddy up at the dam has had seven fish on." At this, I motioned to Burl and the three of us joined Mike at the dam.

I saddled up to Mike to get the scoop and he began giving me the blow-by-blow. He ended by nodding toward the man on his upstream shoulder, then started:

"This guy has been here since morning and hasn't had a touch. Every time I hooked a fish he would shake his head, but wouldn't say anything. After a few more fish I began feeling guilty, so I offered to rig him up. Believe it or not, on his first cast he hooked a fish!"

When the four of us wrapped it up, the score on the Saugeen River was, Noodle Rods 12, Crowd 1. You know who the "1" was? It was Mike's new friend, a fireman from Hamilton, Ontario.

Since that introduction of the noodle rod technique on the Saugeen, one fraternity of Ontario steelheaders opted for a unique method of presenting their roe bags to steelhead. They adopted the English float reel, or center-pin reel to cast their float (bobber).

The reel is palmed to cast and to retrieve, which is very different. Its five inch diameter gives it an automatic "hi-

New York's Salmon River is one of the finest steelhead sites in the country, attracting hundreds of steelheaders from the eastern states.

gear" ratio, making it easier, quicker to cast and to retrieve. However, except for the unique reel, they are just float fishing for steelhead.

While Archie desires the longest rod to drift bobbers, he does not want a three piece rod. This definitely limits my ability to go longer for him. Meanwhile, this growing group of Ontario float boys are reaching up to 17 and 18 foot IMX graphite noodle rods and you can bet I am building these in three pieces. Their preference in fishing such long float rods could also go back to their Motherland, where fishing 20 foot (sectional) rods are traditional. However, I don't believe Englanders fish long rods they can wrap into a "C" with two pound test mono. Noodle rod-lite lining techniques are number one with steelheaders in Ontario, Canada.

In the fall of 1978, I invited the late Bob Peel, former outdoor editor of the Syracuse, New York, newspapers, to fish with Burl and me. We fished our Grand River in Michigan's second largest city, downtown Grand Rapids, and wore out his arms fighting brown trout, coho, chinook, lake trout and steelhead. He returned to Syracuse and wrote about this experience. He then invited us to their Salmon River, in Pulaski, New York. It was to be a spring trip.

Well, one of my many mottos is, "You never leave fish to go look for fish," so we couldn't leave our Michigan streams during prime time for steelhead. This meant we couldn't go until May, even though their runs would be over too. Archie, Burl and I made the trip and Bob made it a very thorough undertaking. The visit and his write-ups encouraged me to accept an invitation to a March, Syracuse sport show.

Burl and I rolled into Syracuse, set up our show display at the State Fair Grounds, grabbed six rods and headed for Black Hole on the Salmon River. We arrived to find three anglers fishing the hole, which was fine with us. We just moved in below them, where the water begins to shallow up.

I selected a 14 foot fiberglass rod and hung a bobber on the eight pound main line. Burl opted for a 10 1/2 footer and

I don't believe there is a month in the year when the famous Niagara River does not yield trout.

bounced the shallower water below me. He propped the spare rods against the cyclone fence behind us. By now, his Nuggets had already become our number one bait, so it wasn't surprising to begin hooking fish. Soon, the late-comers began arriving at the Black Hole.

Once again, it quickly became a pre-show, on-stream clinic, with the Okie himself (Burl), reveling in "preaching the gospel" and putting our extra rods in their hands. It was a real event, with at least four of Burl's new students hooking their first steelhead. By show-time the word was out.

During the four-day show, security people had to ask us and those who were glued to our presentation, to leave, after the show had already closed for the night. Also, anglers who were fishing "our way" would return during the show to testify to others standing at our booth. How's that for unsolicited testimony?

During the four day show, Burl sold over 1,000 packages of Nuggets, I ran out of Berkley two and four pound mono and sold 17,000 Eagle Claw No. 12-14, style 42 hooks. This was to become a repeat for my four year tour to the Syracuse shows. The noodle rod-lite line technique remains number one among wading anglers.

It was in the 60s when a steelheader from St. Charles, Michigan, put me onto the Eagle Claw style 30, No. 12-14, wide bend hooks. Just as I was getting into steelhead seminars and talking about the hooks, Eagle Claw decided the hook wasn't worth the effort and dropped it from their line. The only way to continue getting my much heralded little beauties was to special order them—100,000 per size. Wow! I couldn't afford that kind of money, with four kids and being an under-paid teacher, etc., so I decided to hit up "Daddy Warbucks"—farmer-teacher, Burl Brown.

During the first two years of this partnership, I unloaded 600,000 hooks! It continued to the point where Eagle Claw finally brought the hooks back on-line. They are still avail-

In 1993 my six signature Browning noodle rods sold at the rate of 652 per month...in 1994, 743 per month.

able in sport shops, because they are the most popular. The noodle rod-lite lining beat goes on!

The most recent indicator of how well the noodle rods are faring, comes as a result of another avenue of marketing my noodle rod design.

On November 1, 1991, Clarence White, a Michigan tackle "rep" had Kent Heitz, of Browning Fishing Division, join me on the Betsie River. However, a small blizzard forced us into a local restaurant to discuss Browning producing my designed noodle rods.

Kent forwarded the prototypes to me for suggestions and since they were on the nose, I returned them with high hopes that Browning could come up with a price which would allow the first true-designed manufactured noodle rod to compete in the market place. After all, not everyone can afford to order my custom built rods. In a few weeks I received word from Kent, "It's a go!"

There are now three rods in Browning's traditional Medallion series and three in their Hi-Power series. More specifically, there is a nine foot rod, designed for four to six pound test in both series', a 10 1/2 foot rod, designed for two to four pound test in both series' and an 11 1/2 foot rod, designed for two to four pound test in both series.

October 31, 1993 ended their first year on the market and the total number of these rods sold in the U.S. and Canada came to slightly less than 7,000. I can only assume this means the six signature noodle rods are a big success, since Browning has me designing two more. These two will be seven and eight foot ultra-lites.

Another late indicator on the welfare of the noodle rod, lite-lining technique, is the overwhelming response to my new video cassette, "chinook-Steelhead", which I mentioned earlier. If seeing is more believing than reading, it is the only two part video addressing these two most popular species of fish in the Great Lakes.

In the early 1980s, a Washington-based magazine, *Fishing Holes*, corresponded with me about the results of our summer trips and the noodle rod technique. As a result, one of the editors penned an article, "Noodle Rods—Breakthrough or Ultra-Light Fad?"

While this very informative fishing magazine has gone the way of many magazines, noodlin' for steelhead and salmon is still going strong!